VOLCANO
volcanoes around the world

Here's the list of volcanic locations :

Mount Fuji — Japan
Kilauea — Hawaii, USA
Mount Etna — Sicily, Italy
Volcán de Fuego — Guatemala
Eyjafjallajökull — Iceland
Mount Stromboli — Italy
Mount Vesuvius — Italy
Mount St. Helens — USA
Mount Mayon — Philippines
Sakurajima — Japan
Mount Erebus — Antarctica
Erta Ale — Ethiopia
Mount Bromo — Indonesia
Villarrica — Chile
Mount Teide — Canary Islands, Spain
Popocatépetl — Mexico
Cotopaxi — Ecuador
Mount Ngauruhoe — New Zealand
Mount Ruapehu — New Zealand
Mount Pinatubo — Philippines
Kamchatka Peninsula — Russia
Arenal Volcano — Costa Rica
Mount Rainier — USA
Santorini — Greece
Nyiragongo — Democratic Republic of Congo

Anak Krakatau — Indonesia
Mount Merapi — Indonesia
Mauna Loa — Hawaii, USA
Galápagos Islands — Ecuador
Pacaya — Guatemala
Mount Rinjani — Indonesia
Mount Aso — Japan
Taal Volcano — Philippines
Reunion Island — France
Krafla — Iceland
Lake Kawaguchi — Japan
Piton de la Fournaise — Reunion Island
Surtsey — Iceland
Mount Taranaki — New Zealand
Mount Tambora — Indonesia
Mount Agung — Bali, Indonesia
Ol Doinyo Lengai — Tanzania
Mount Yasur — Vanuatu
Mount Ararat — Turkey
Kīlauea — Hawaii, USA
Mount Hekla — Iceland
Mount Kilimanjaro — Tanzania
Mount Elbrus — Russia
Fagradalsfjall — Iceland
Mount Baker — USA

Welcome to Volcanic Wonders, a unique magazine that takes you on a breathtaking journey across the globe to explore the awe-inspiring power and beauty of volcanoes. From the fiery eruptions of Hawaii's Kilauea to the serene majesty of Japan's Mount Fuji, this magazine delves deep into the world's most iconic volcanic landscapes.

Each issue is filled with high-quality imagery, expert insights, and captivating stories about the history, geology, and cultural significance of volcanoes in various countries. Whether you're a seasoned traveler, a nature enthusiast, or simply fascinated by the earth's raw power, Volcanic Wonders will ignite your curiosity and deepen your appreciation for these natural marvels.

Join us as we explore the peaks, craters, and fiery flows of the planet's most majestic volcanoes.

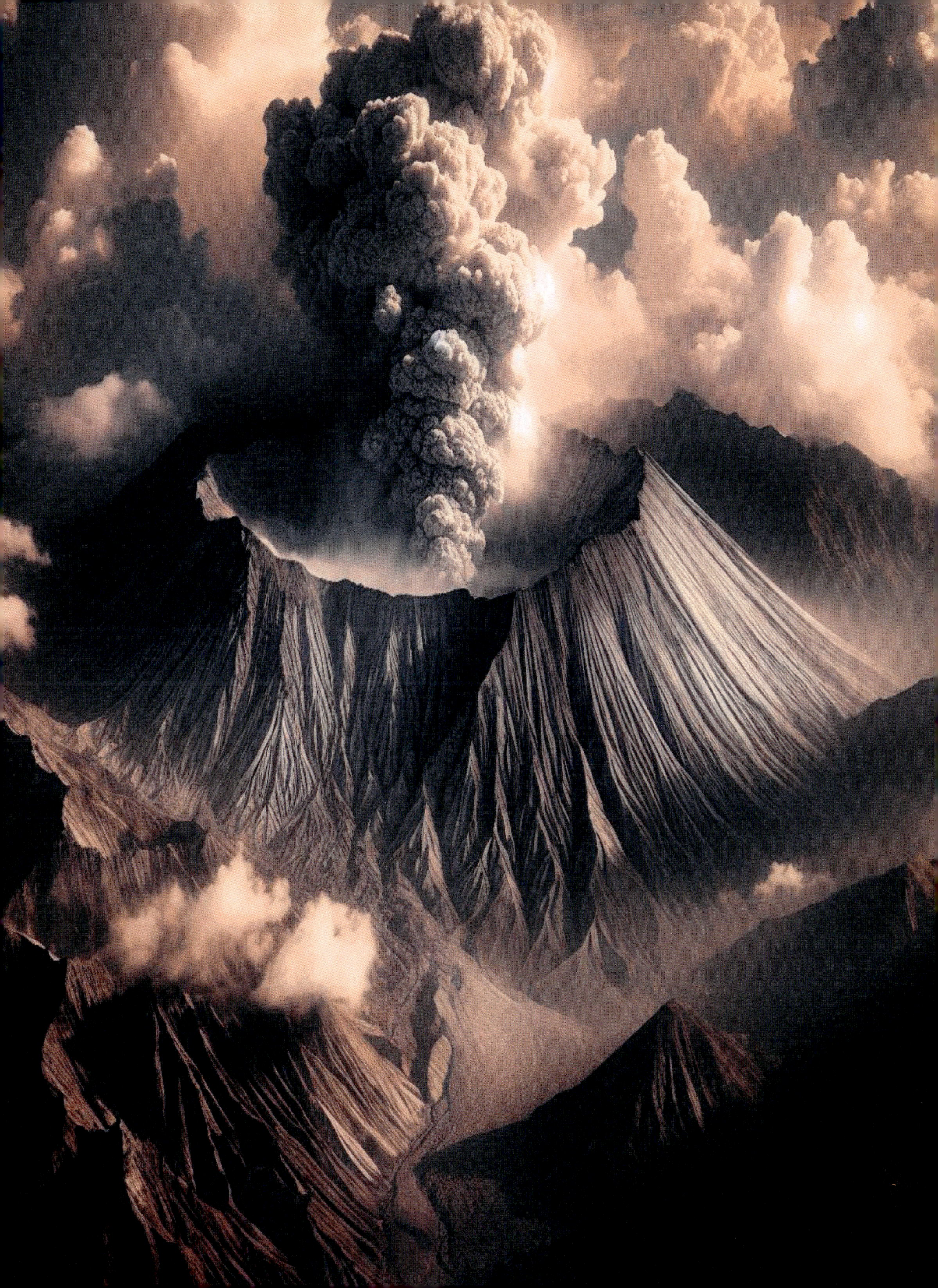

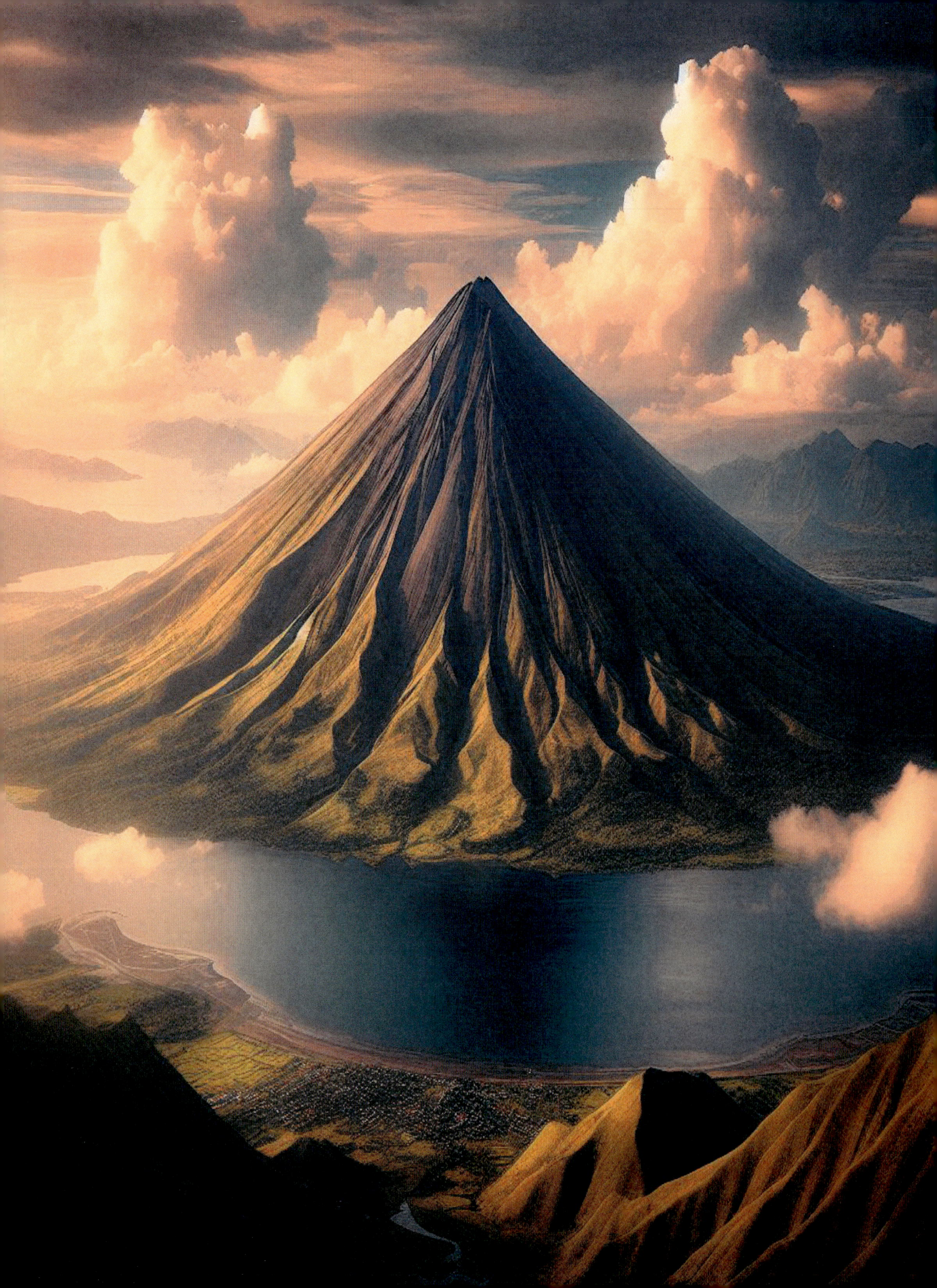

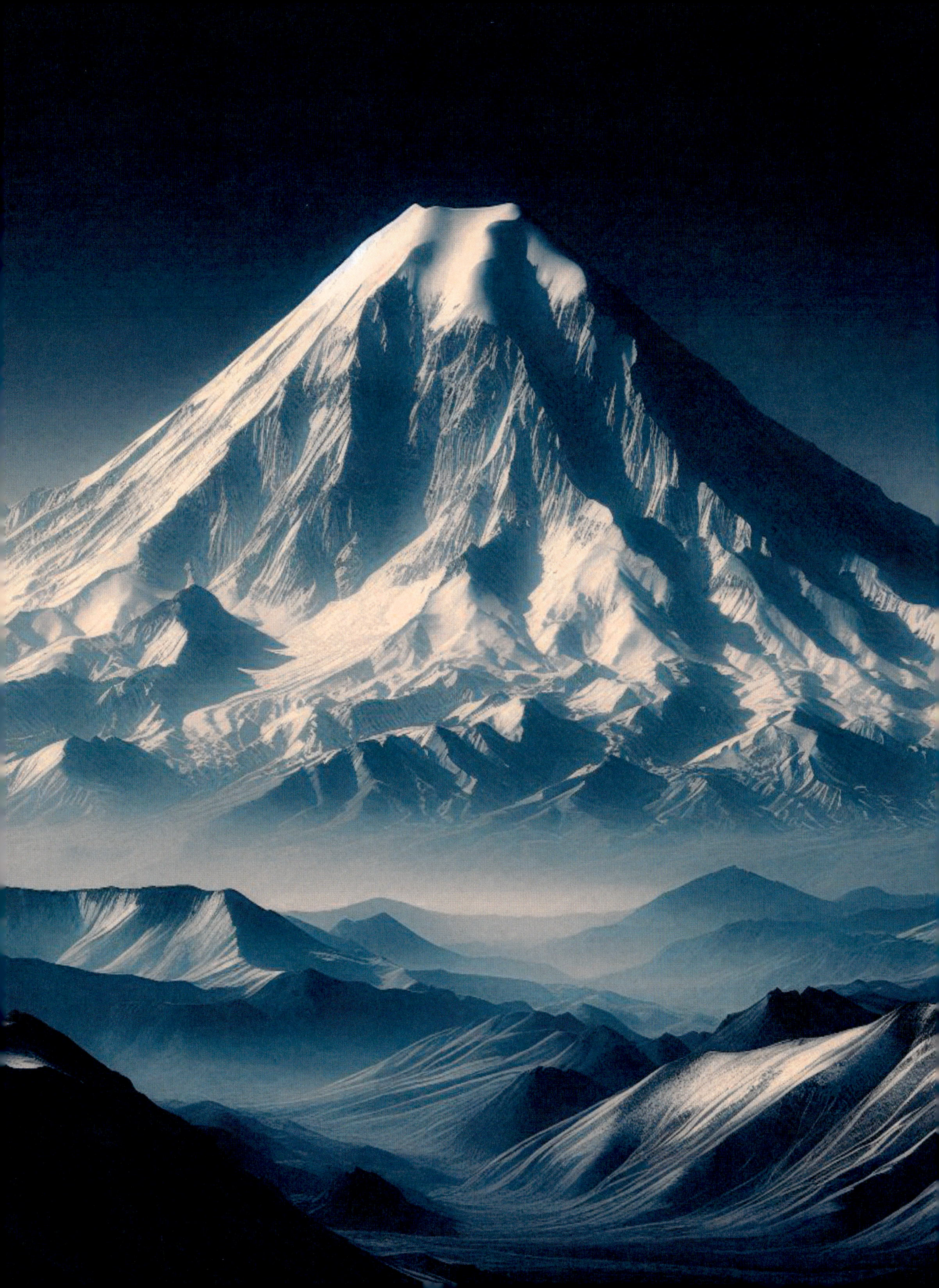

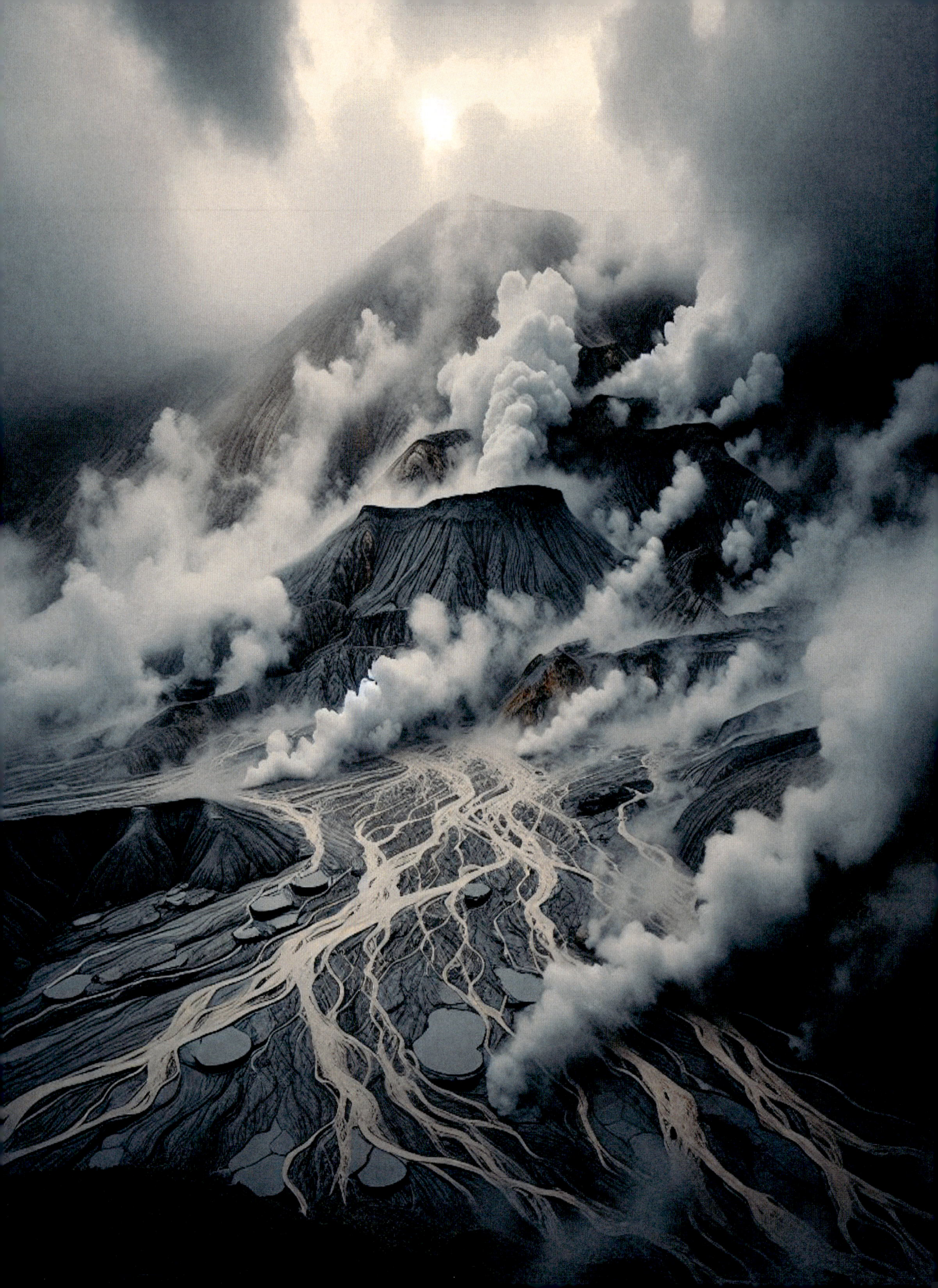

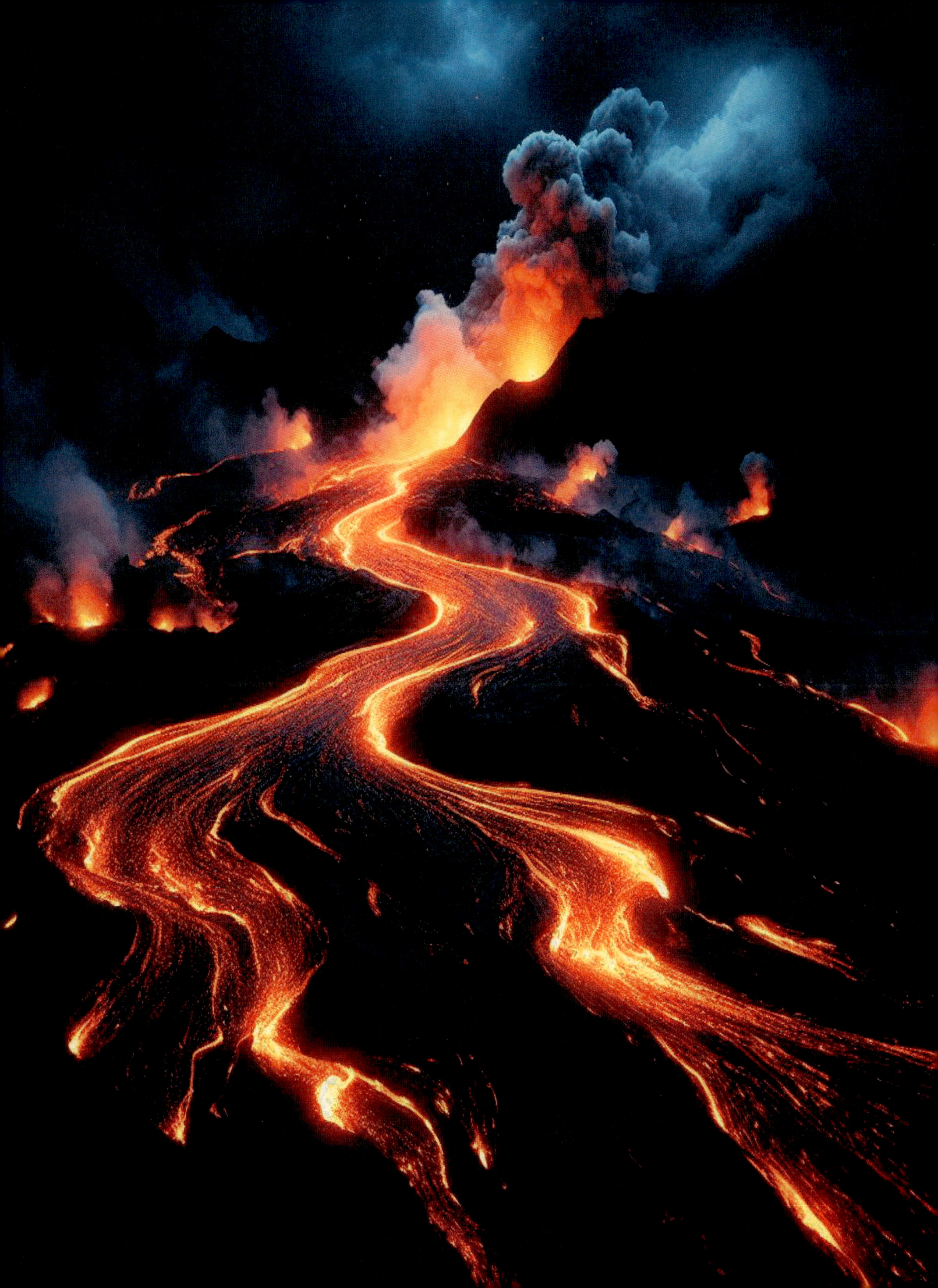

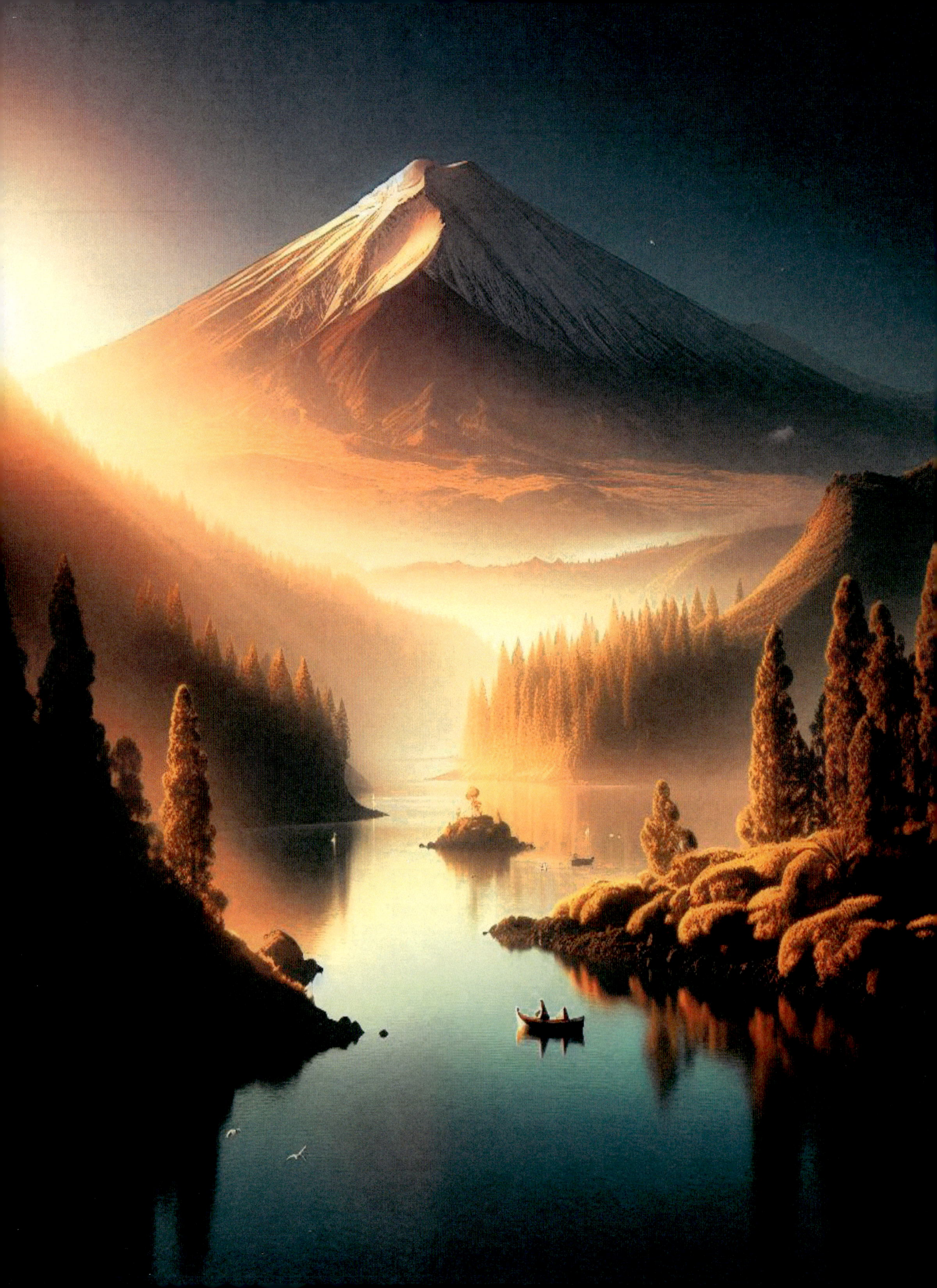

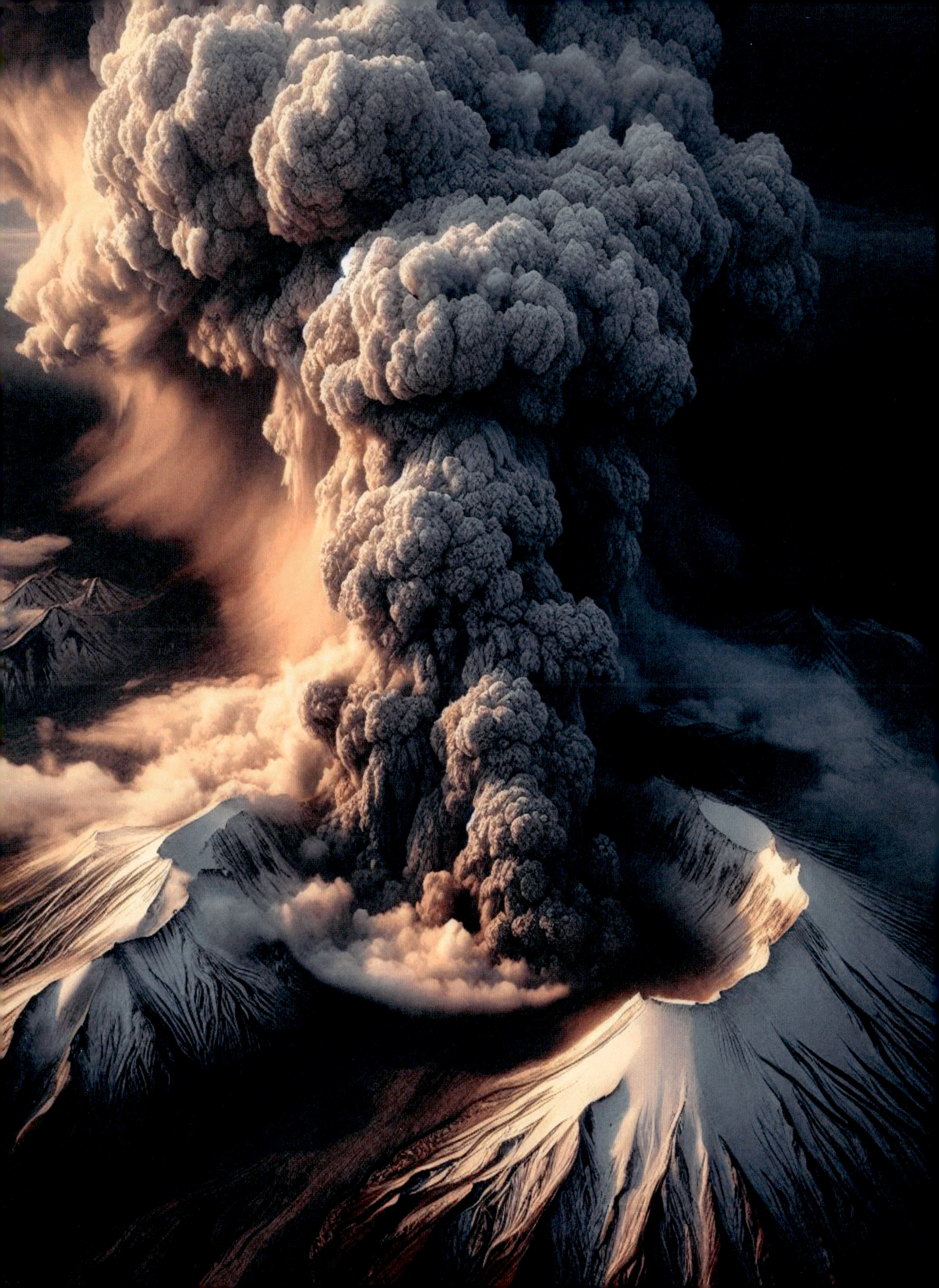

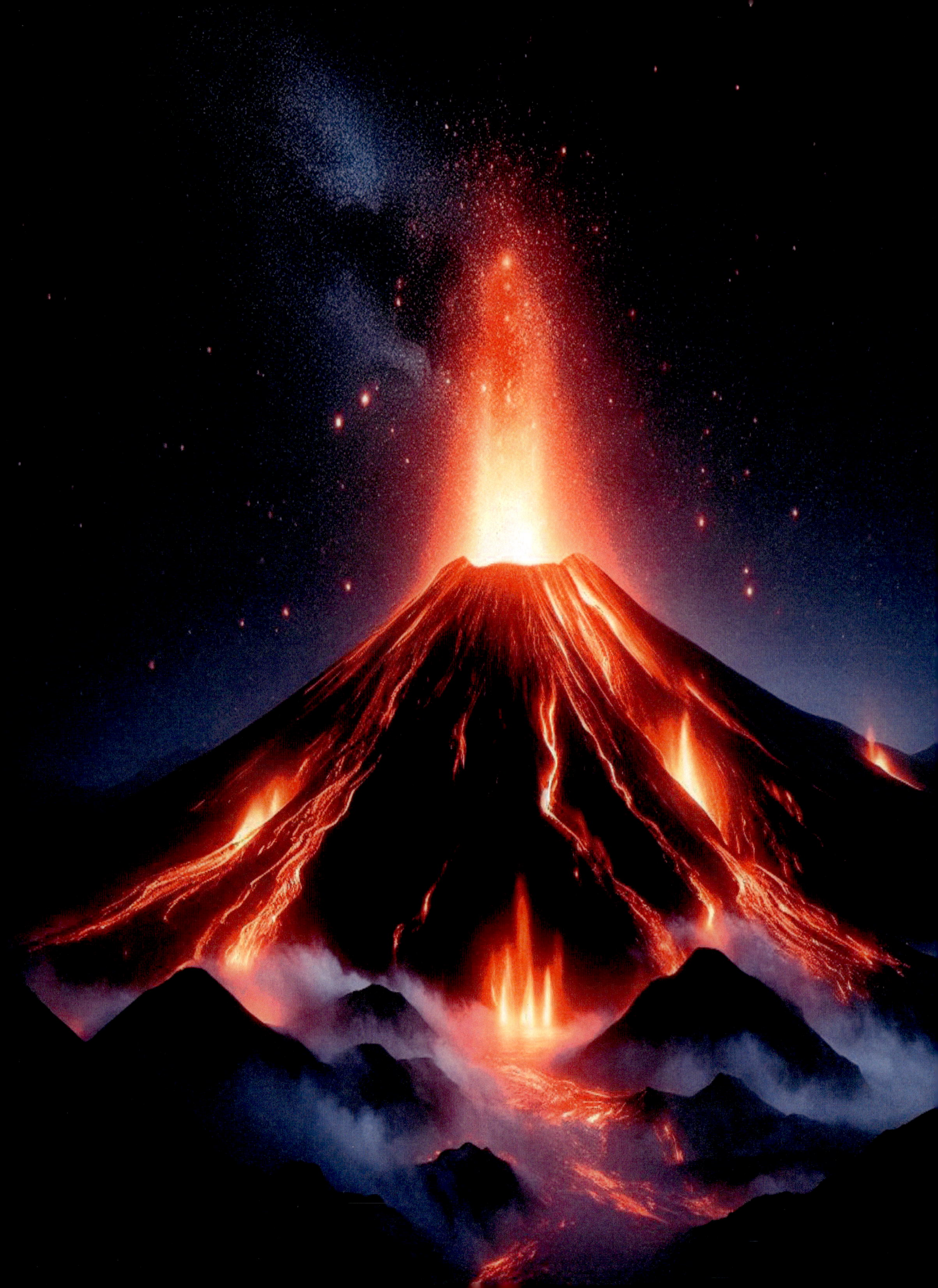

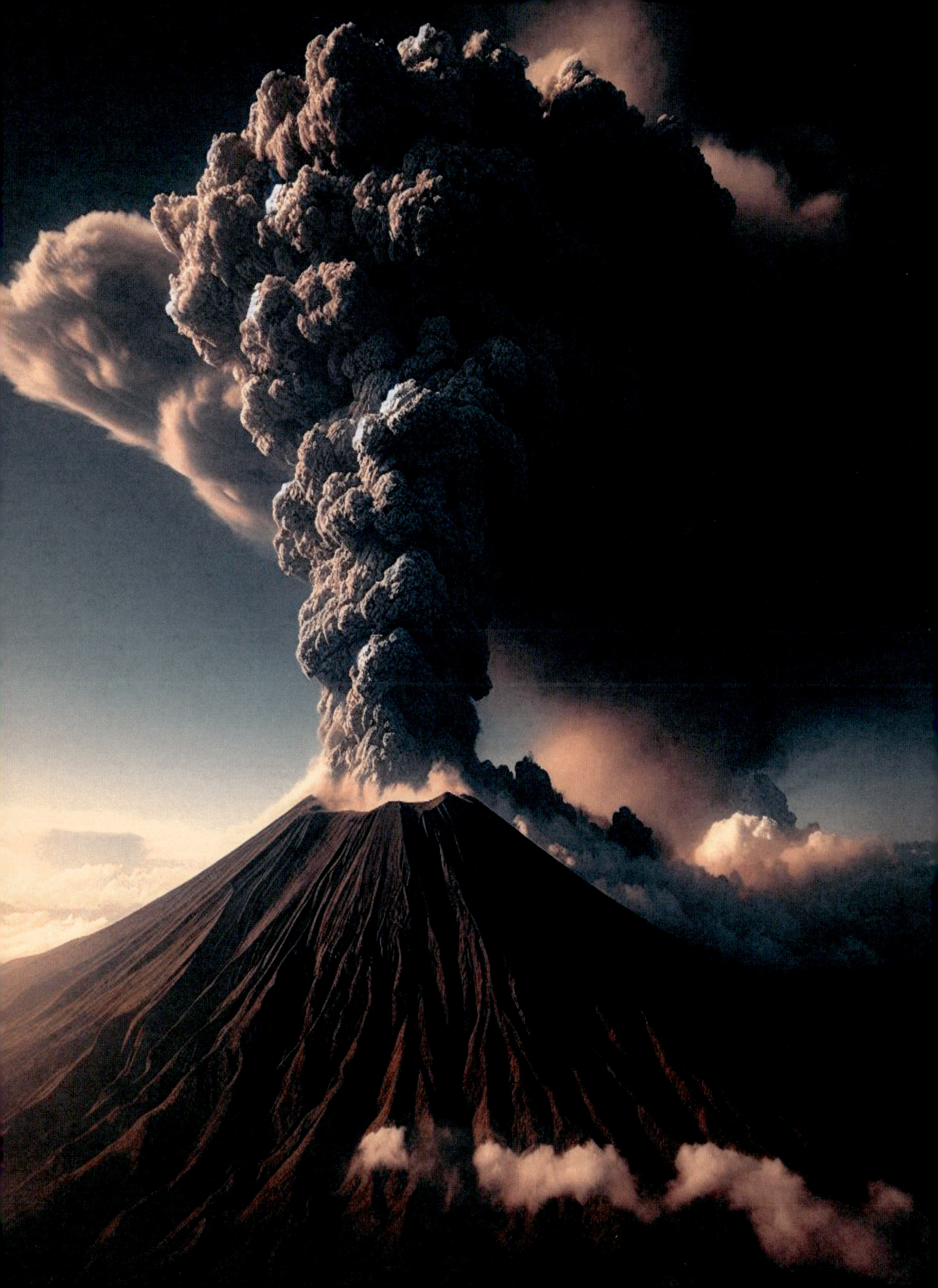

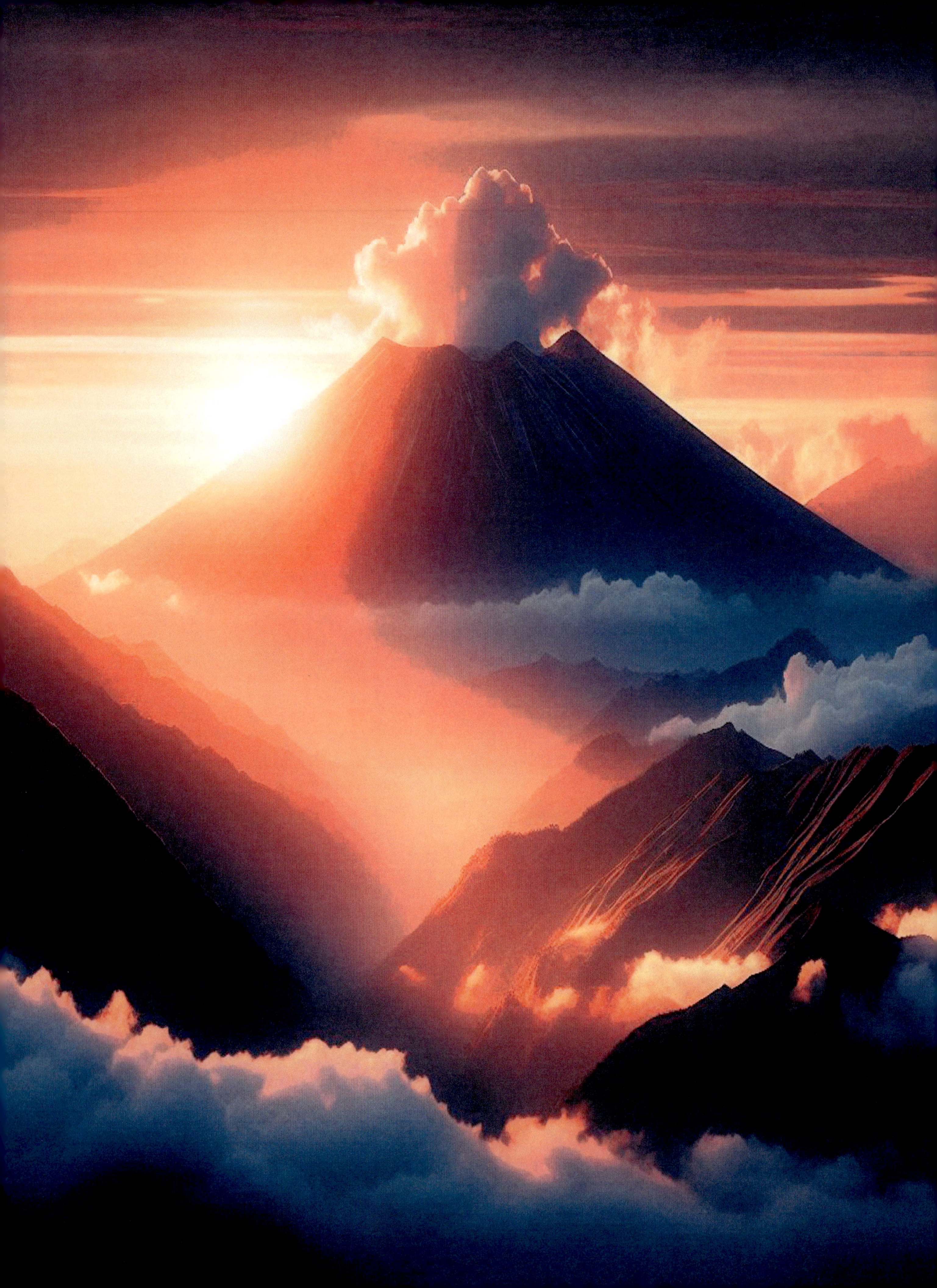

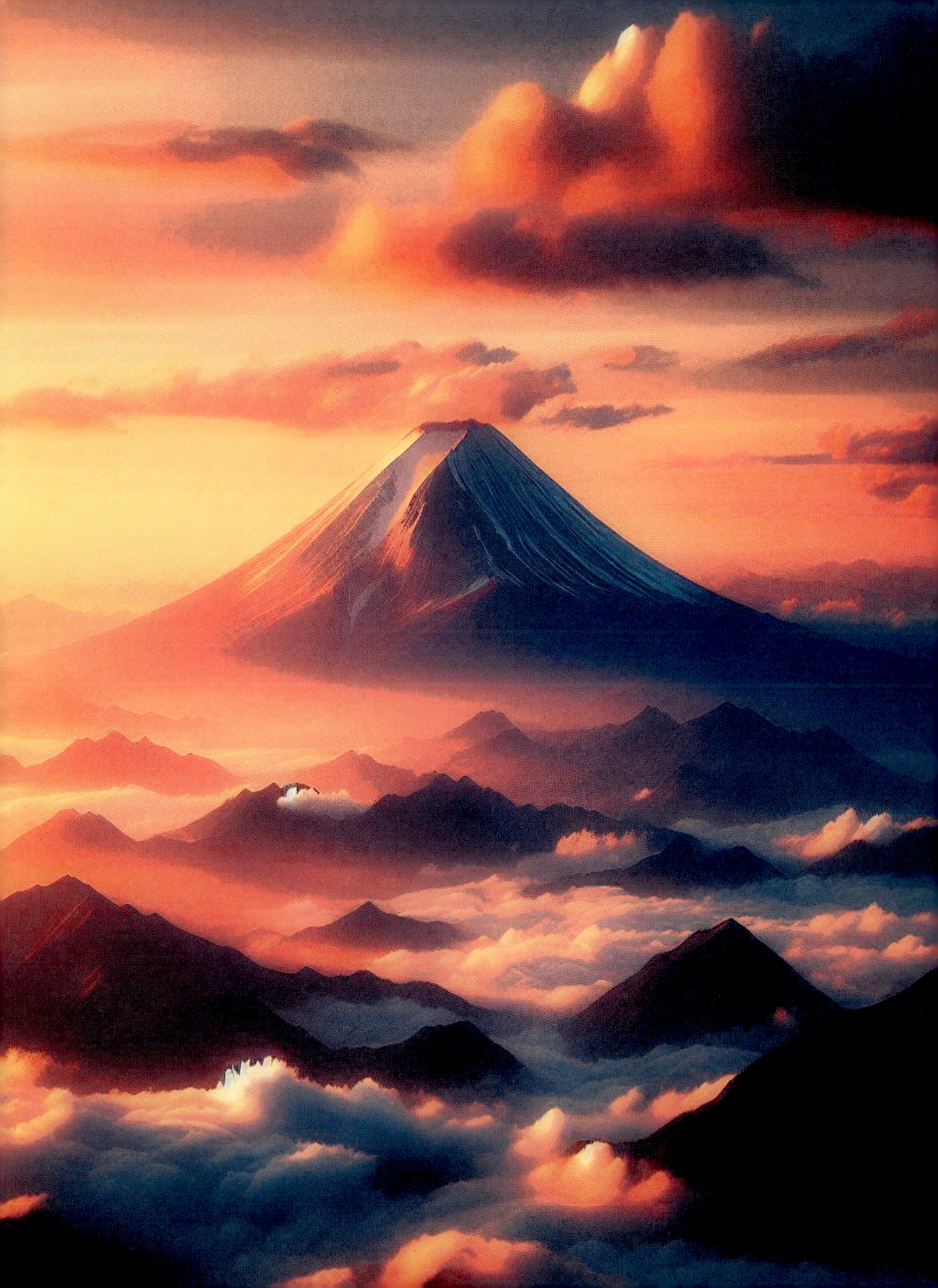

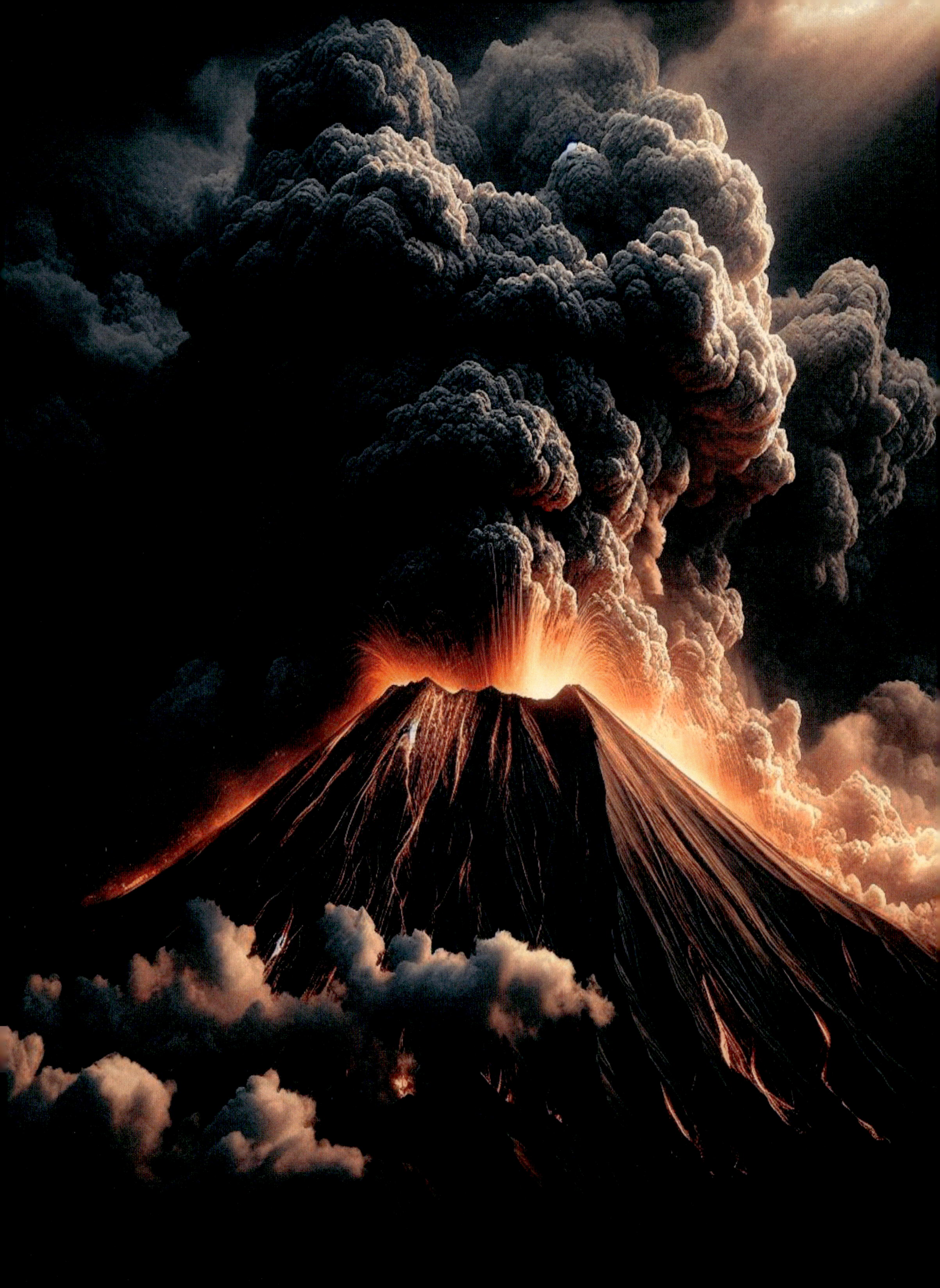

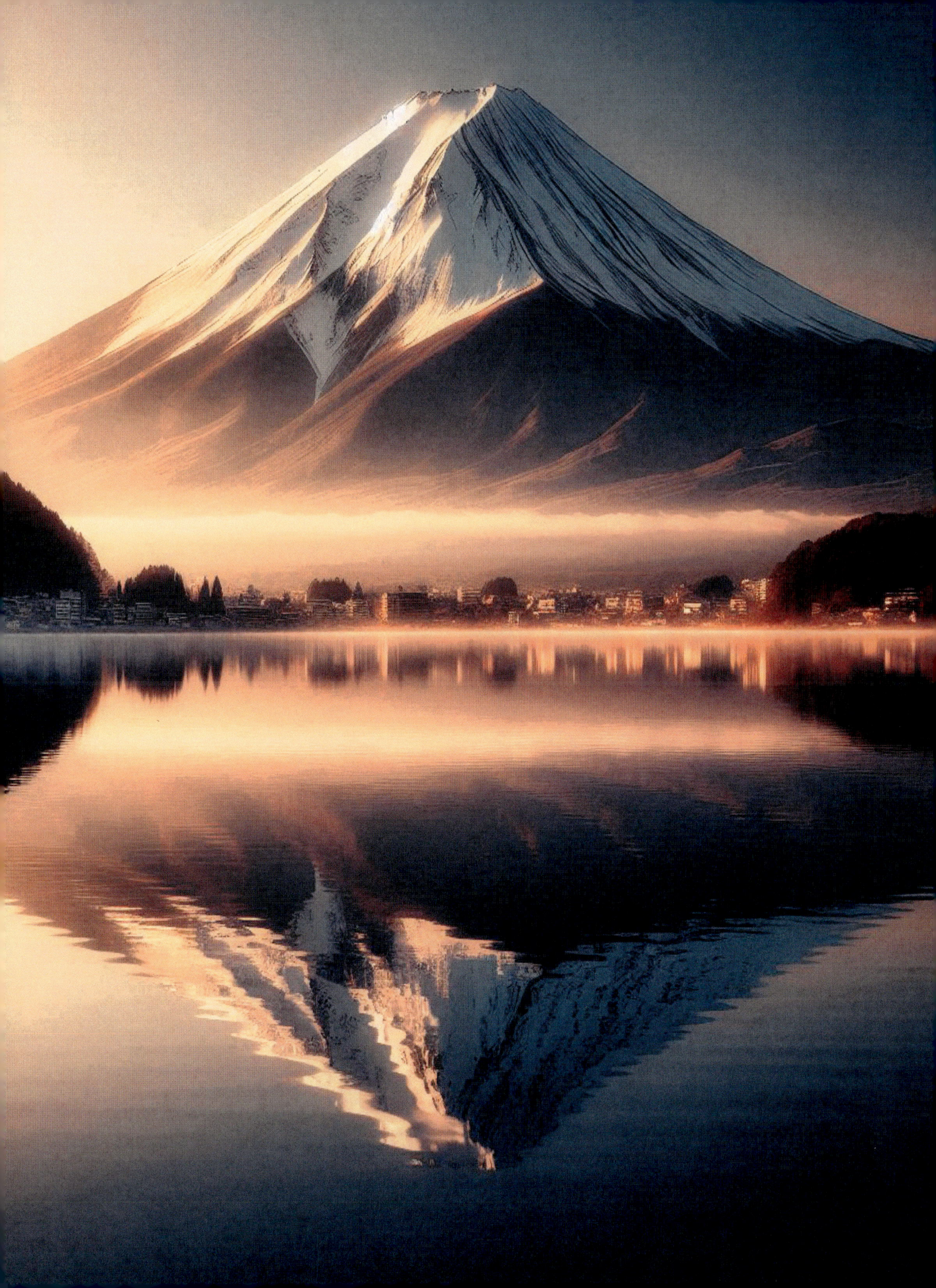

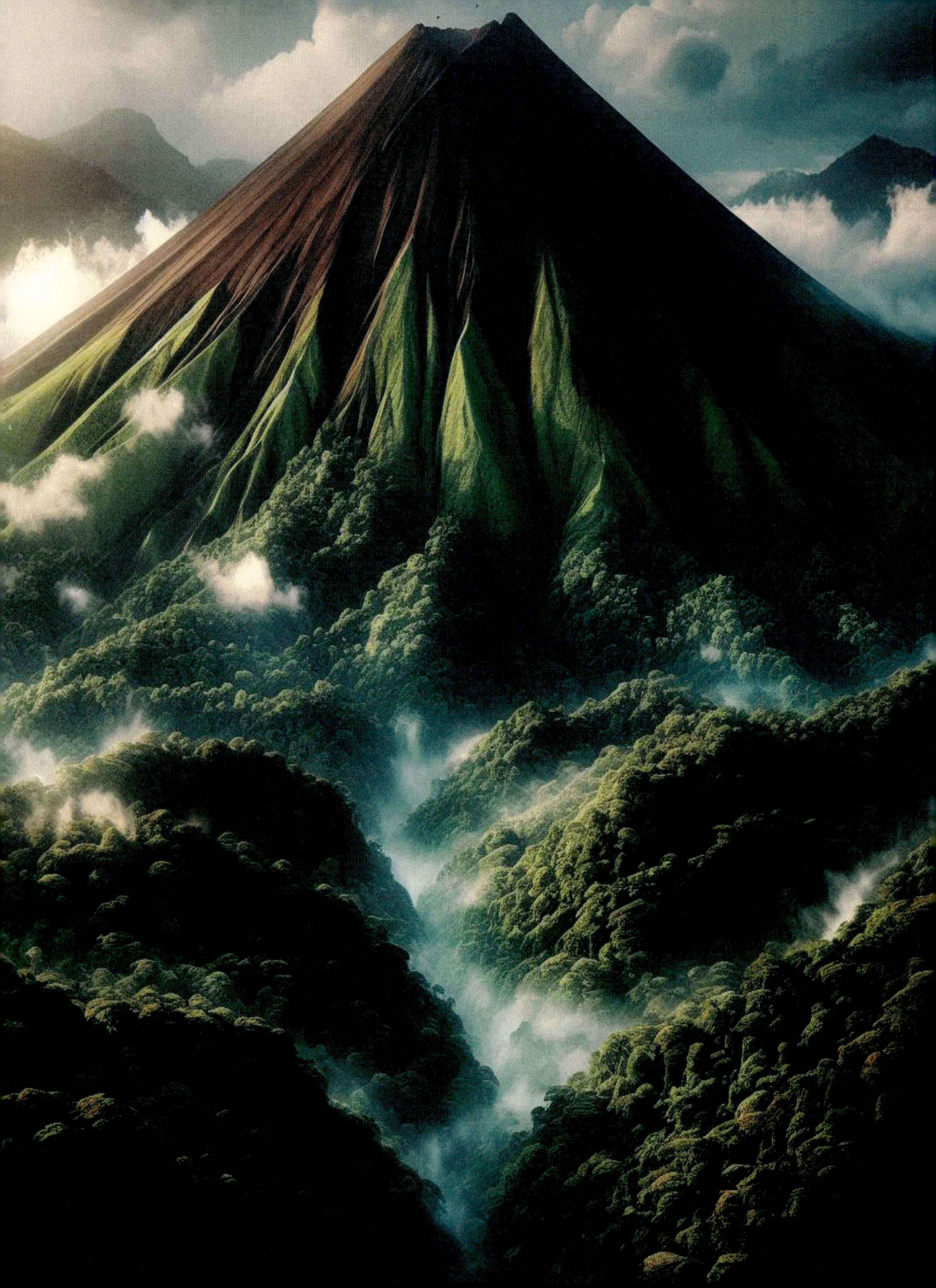

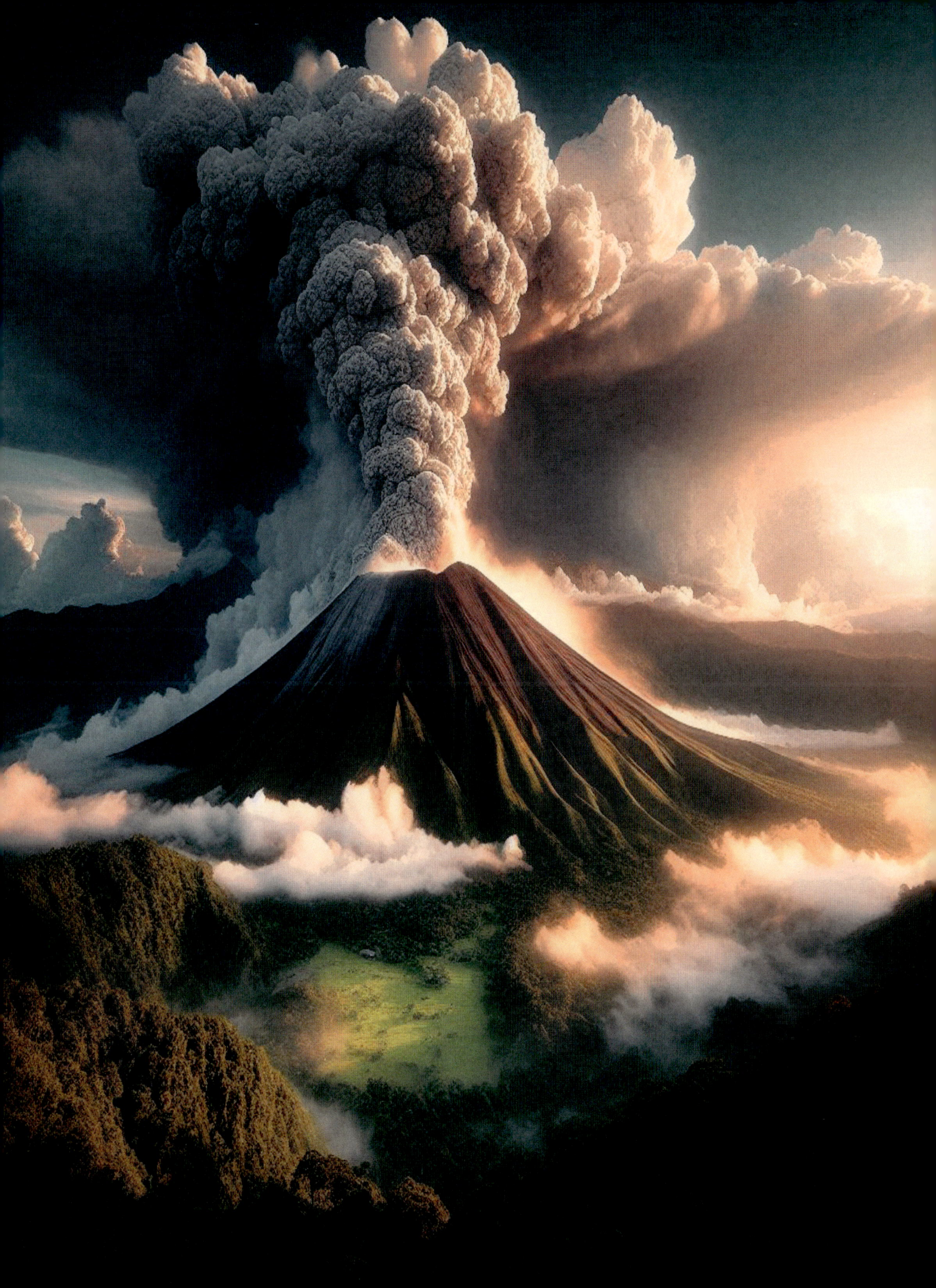

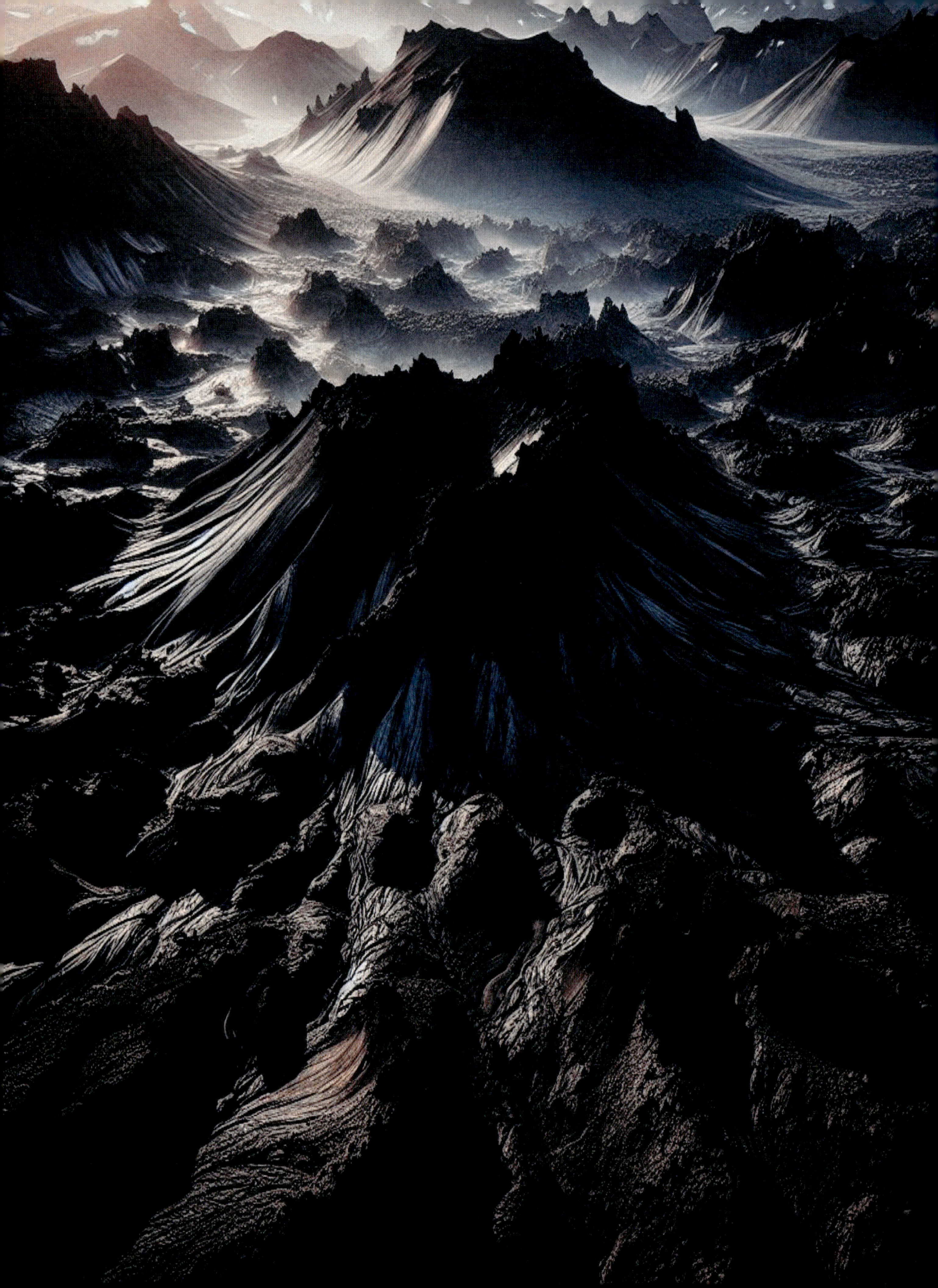

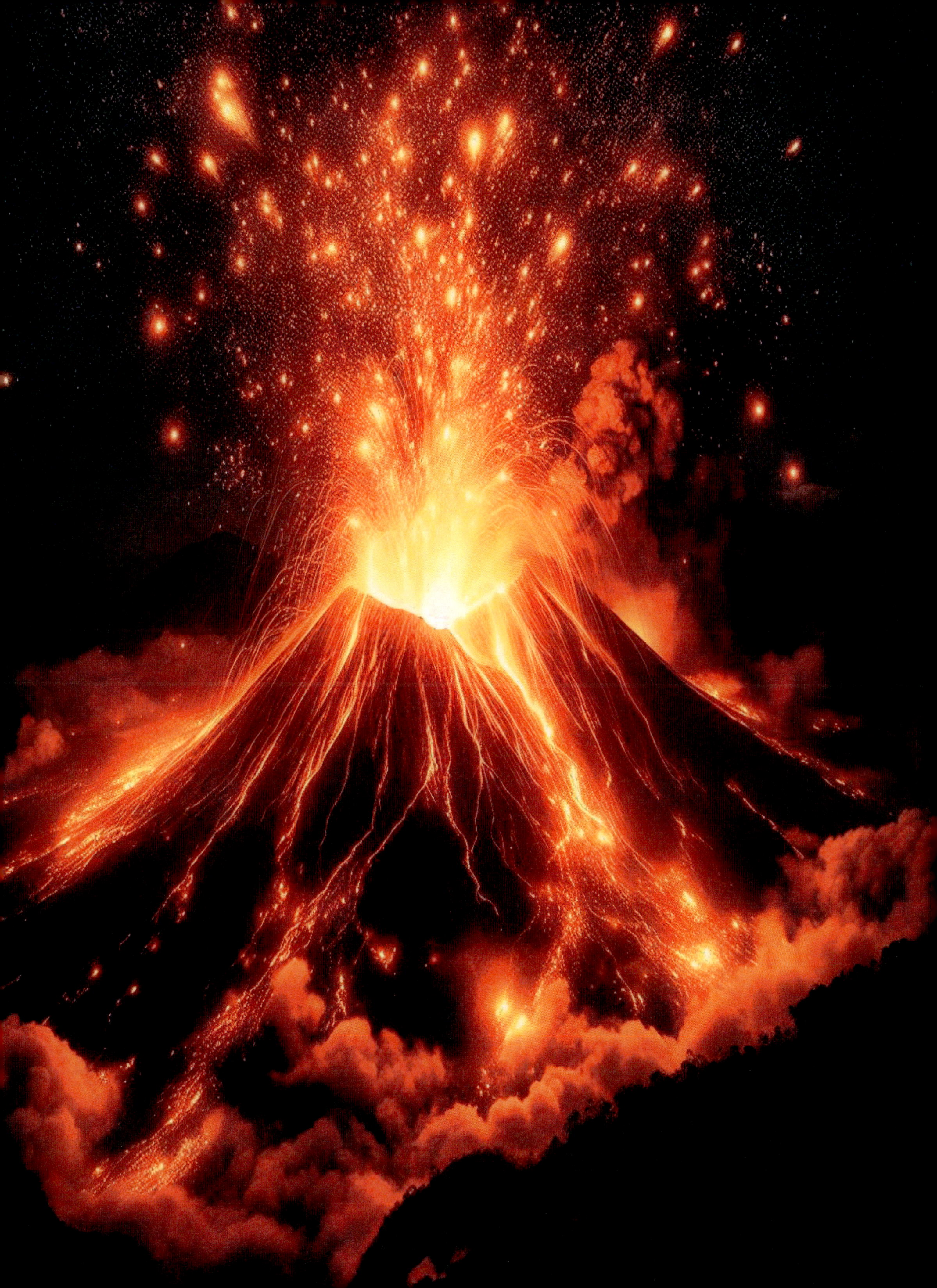

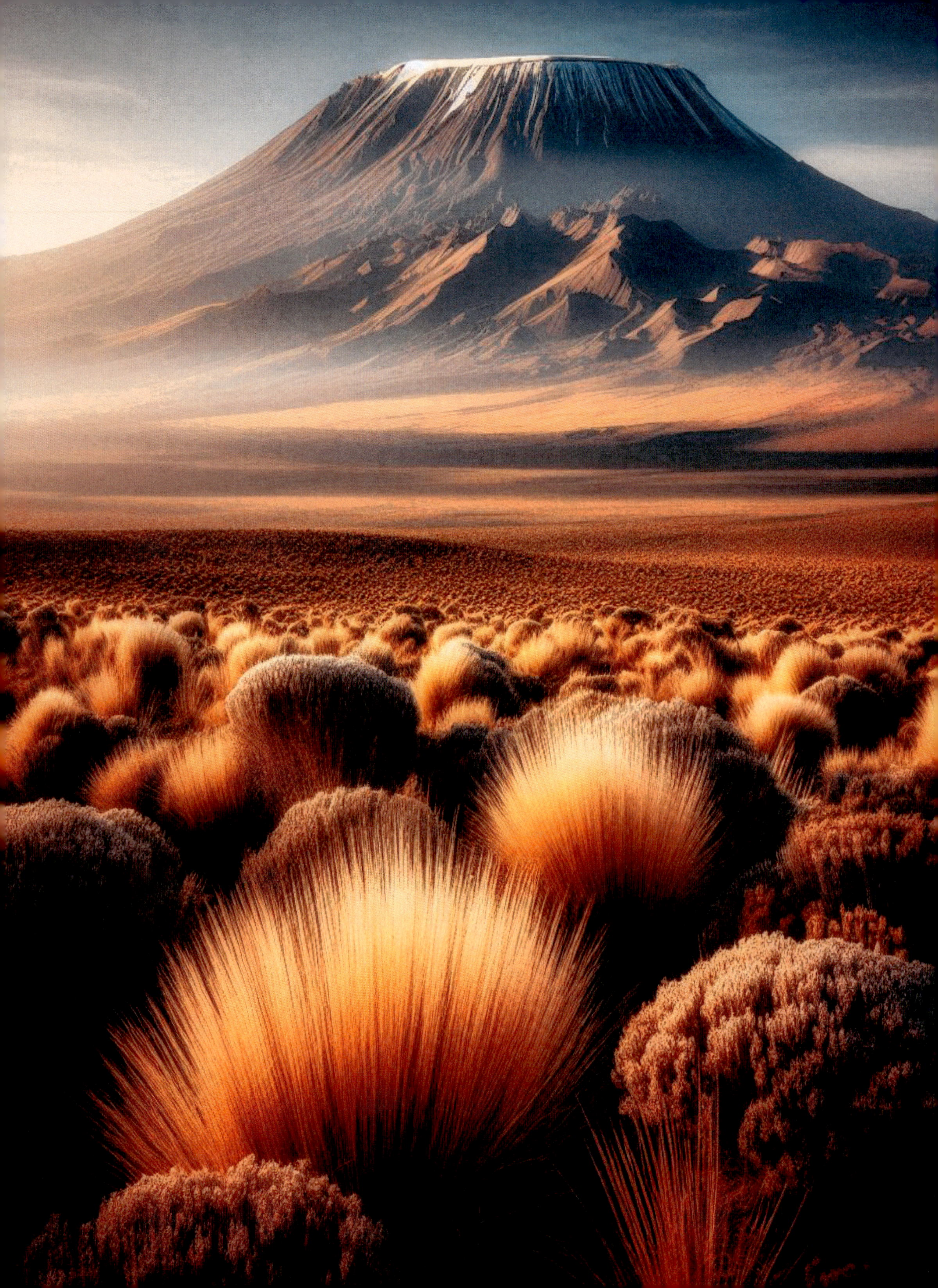

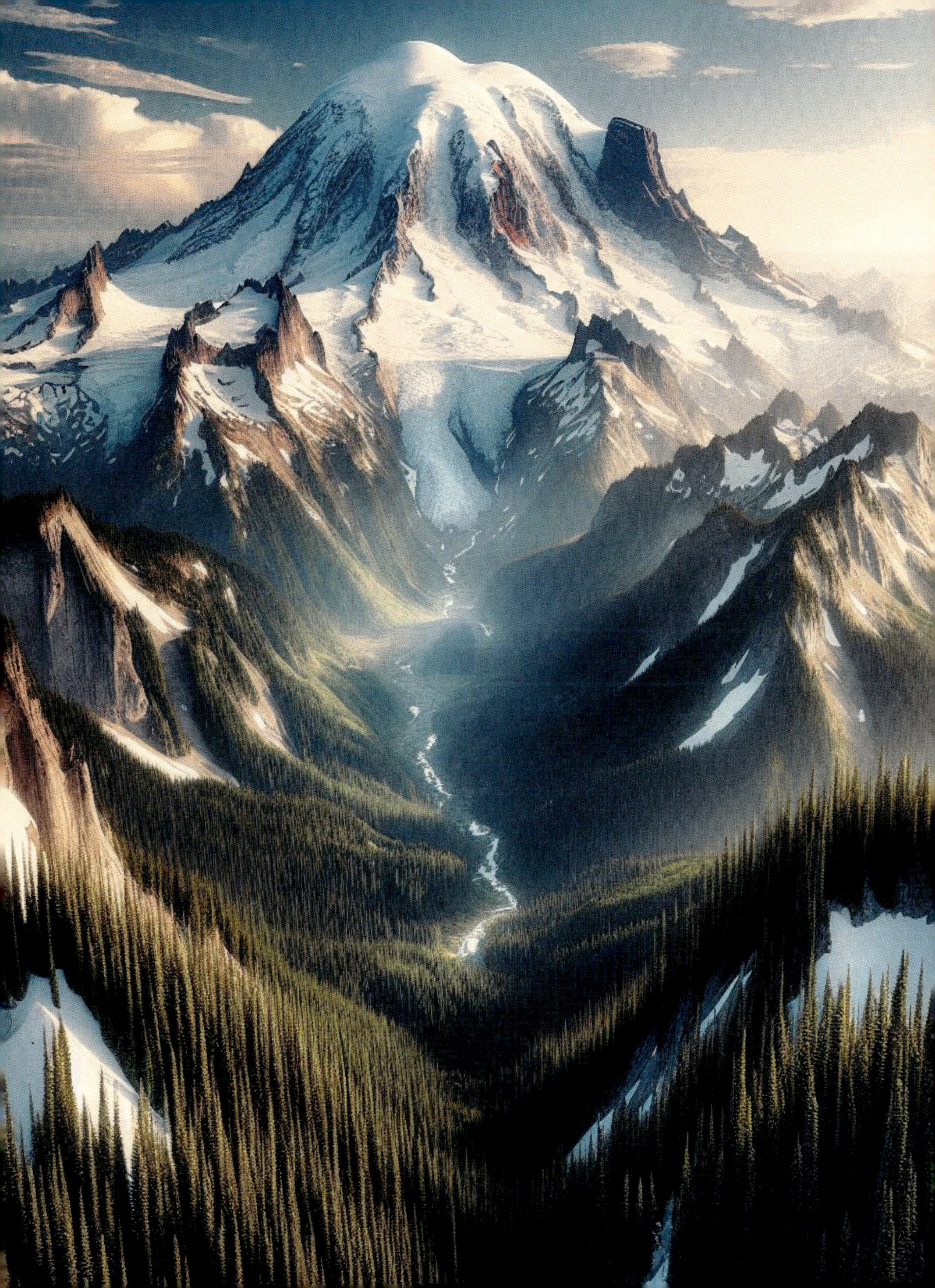

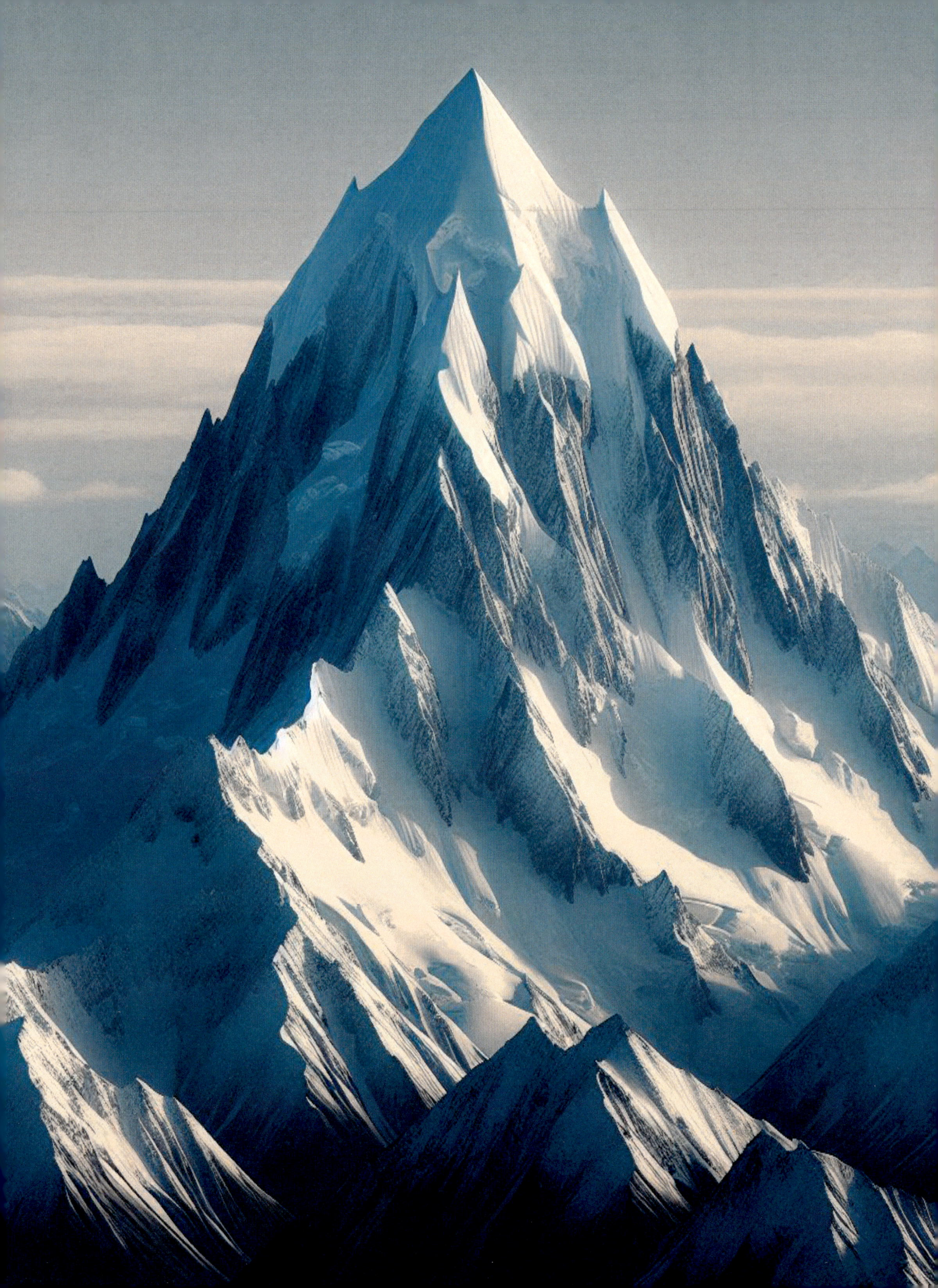

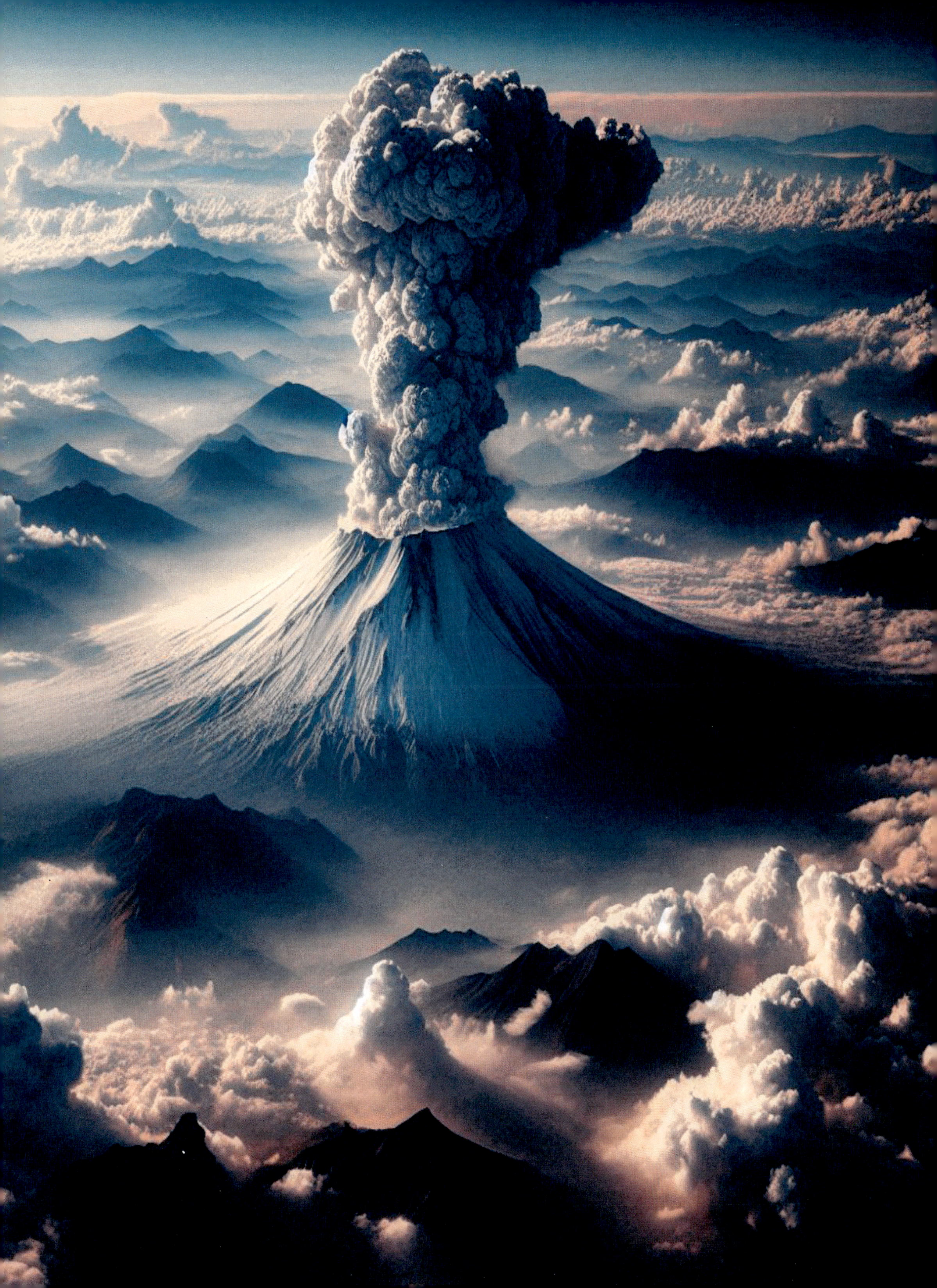

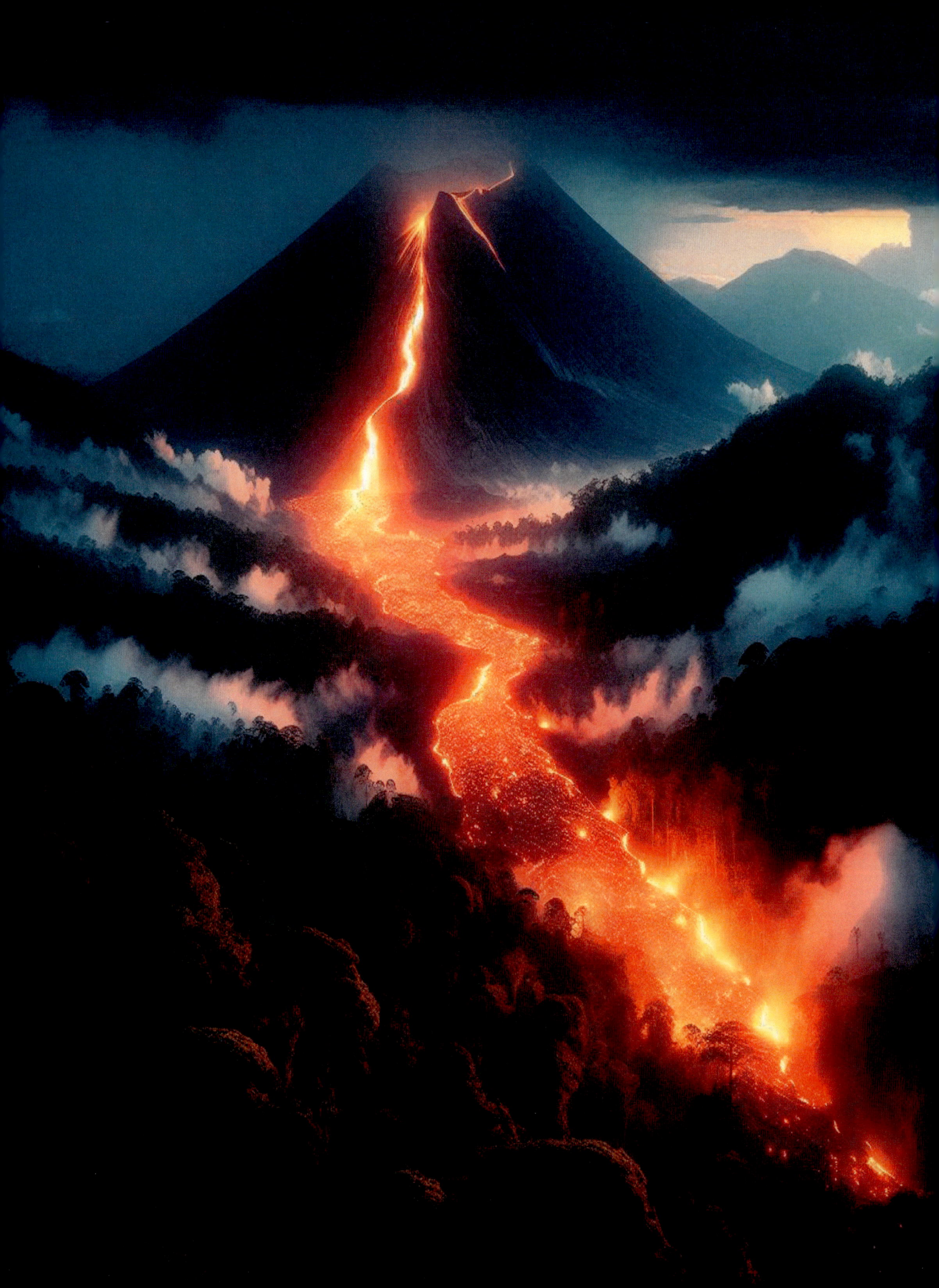

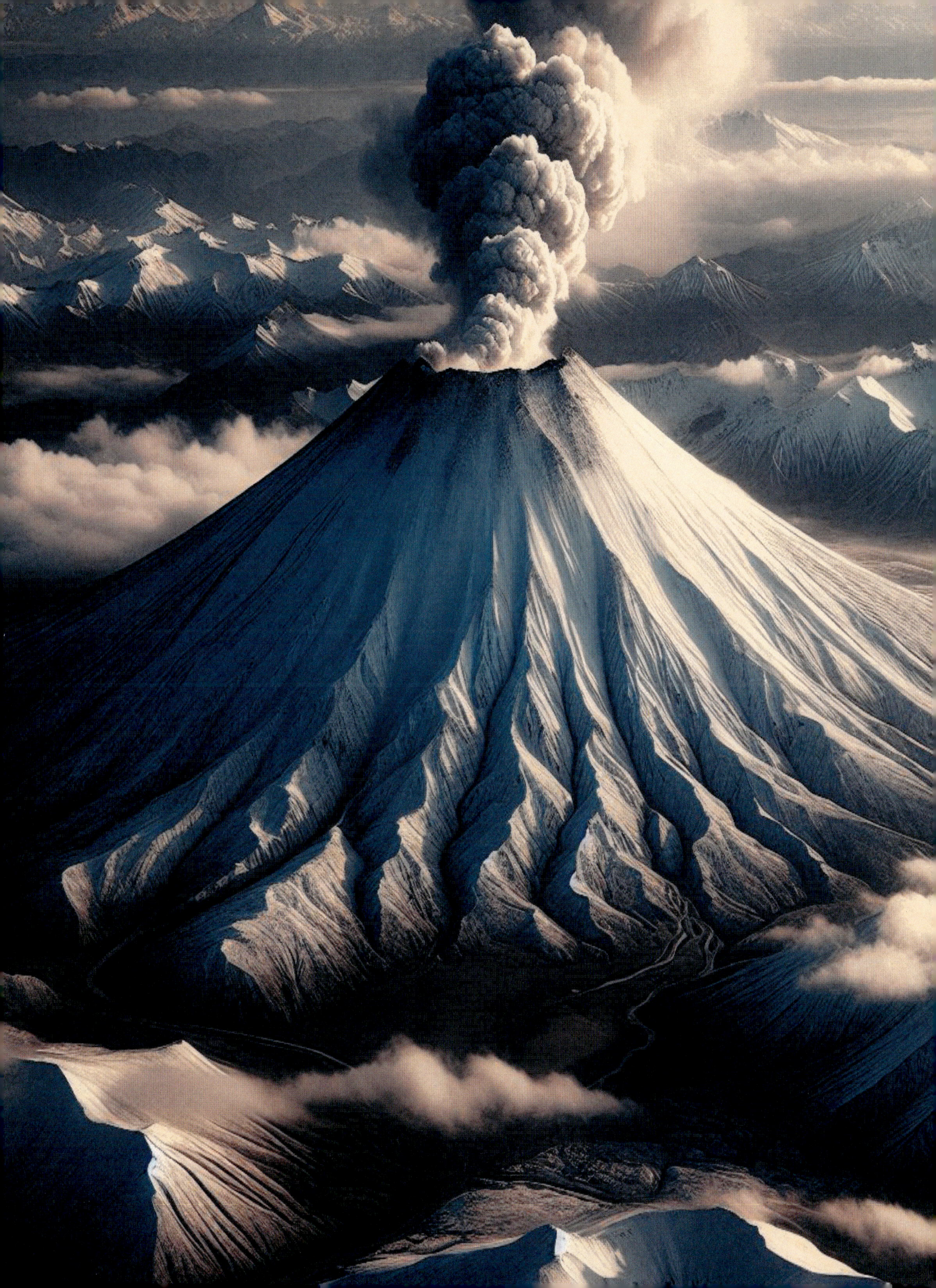

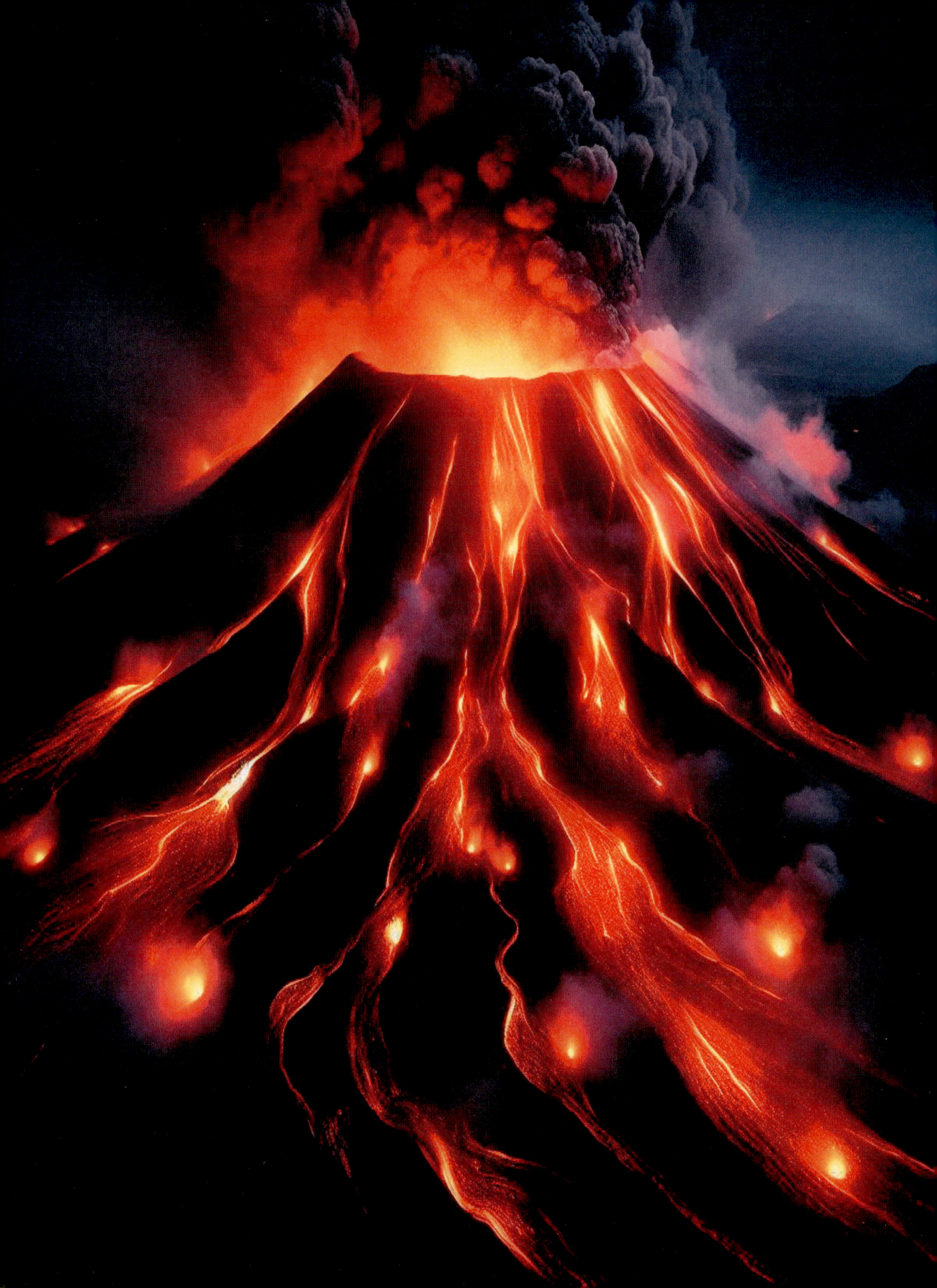

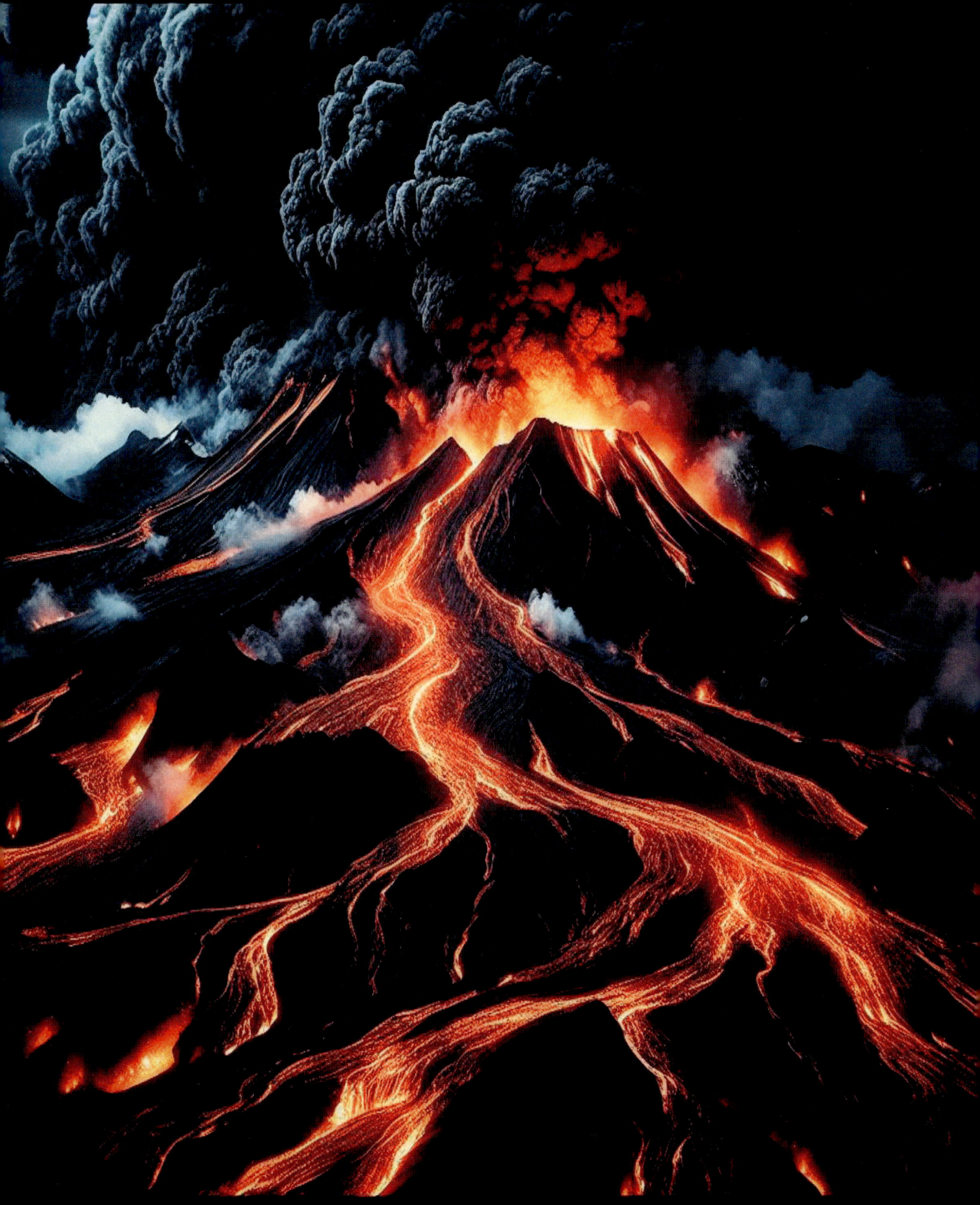

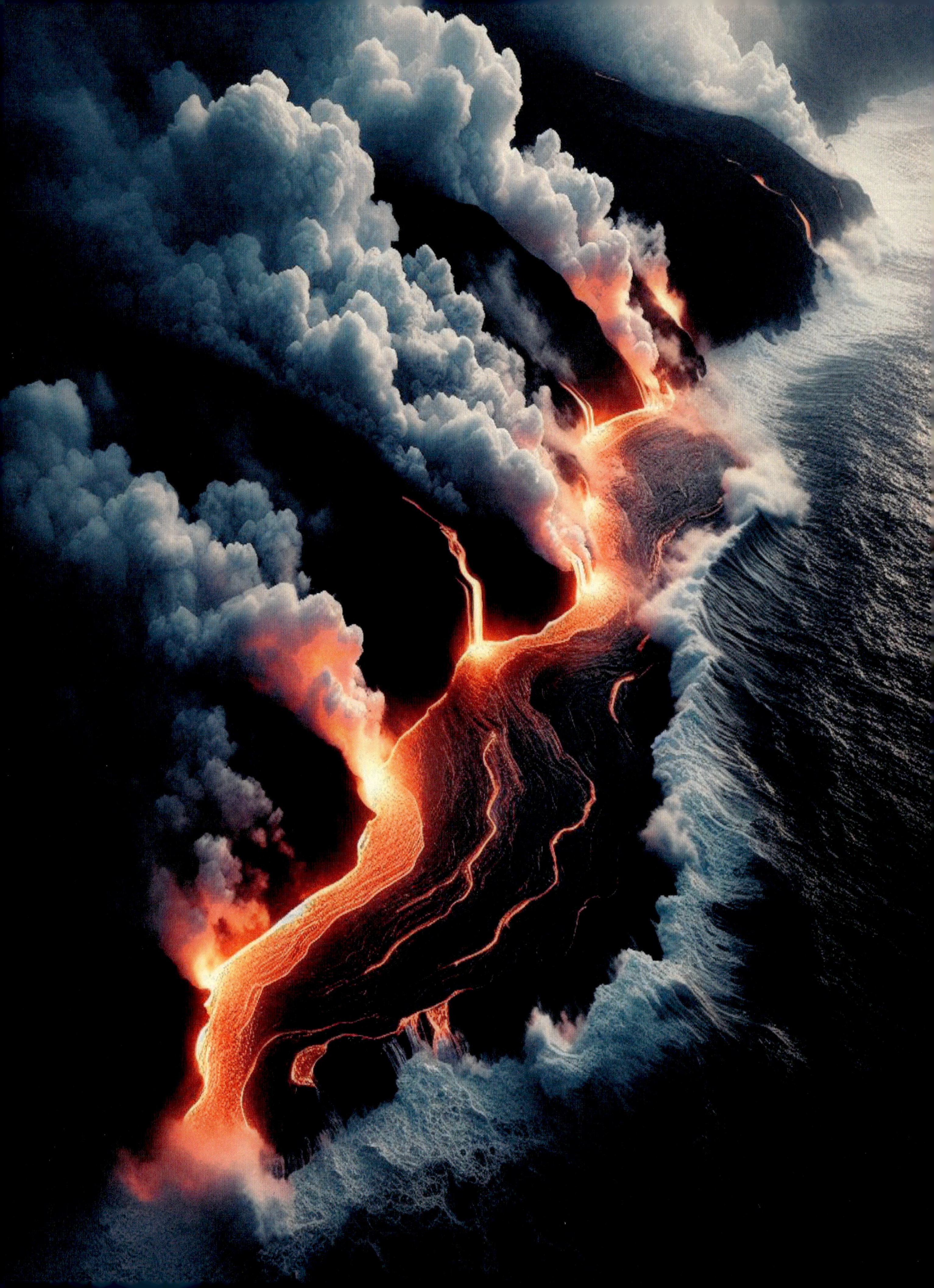

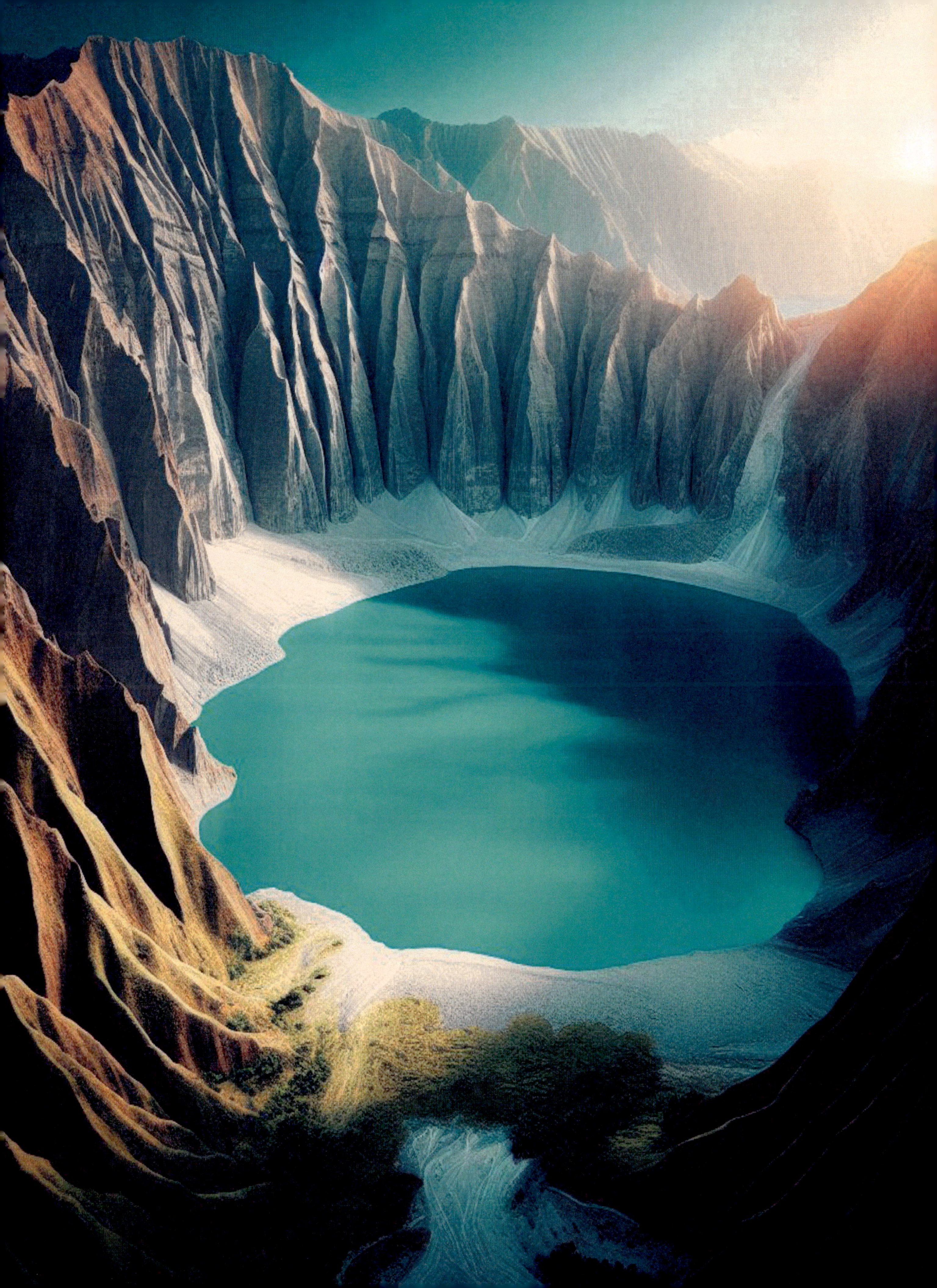

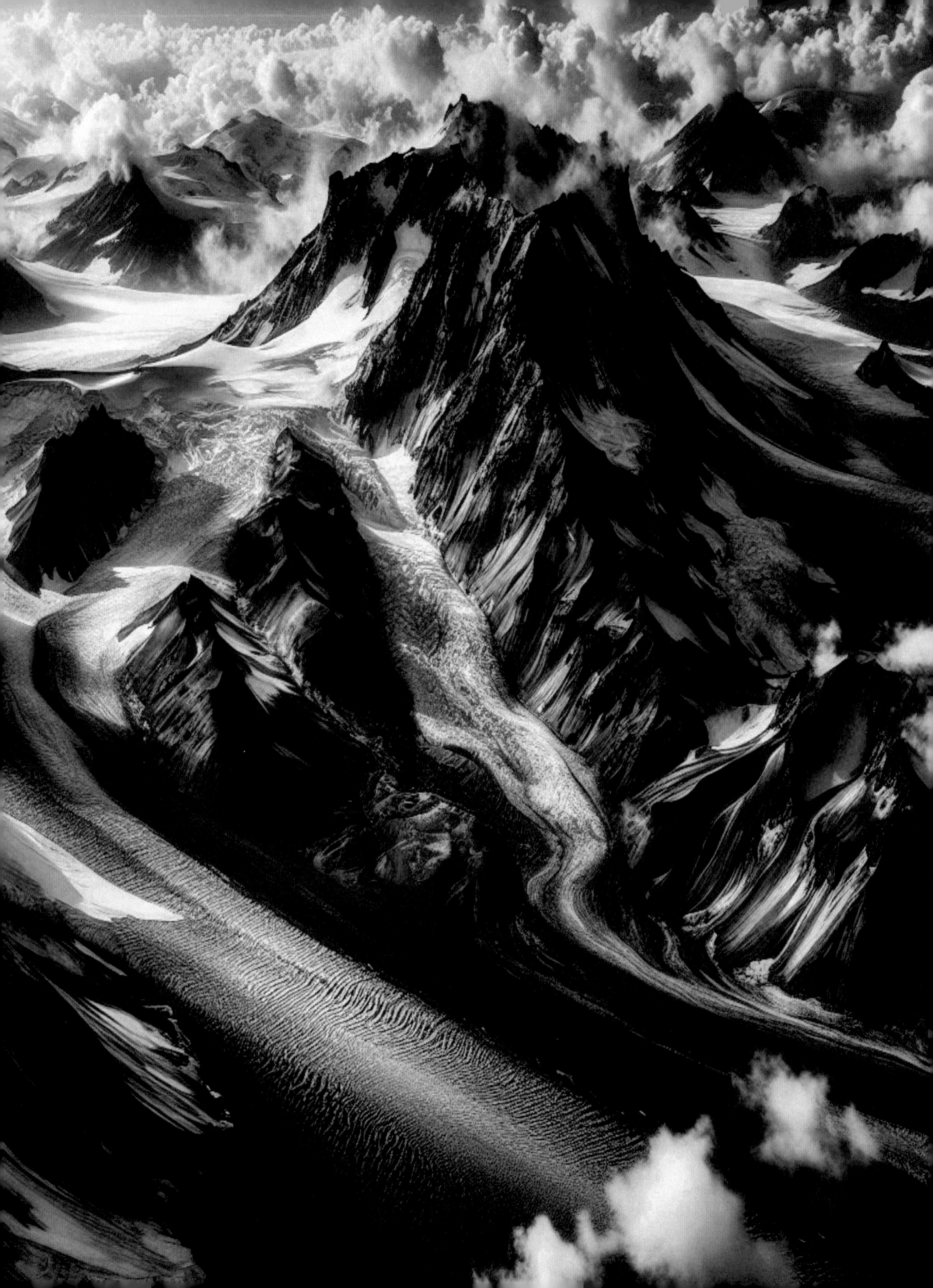

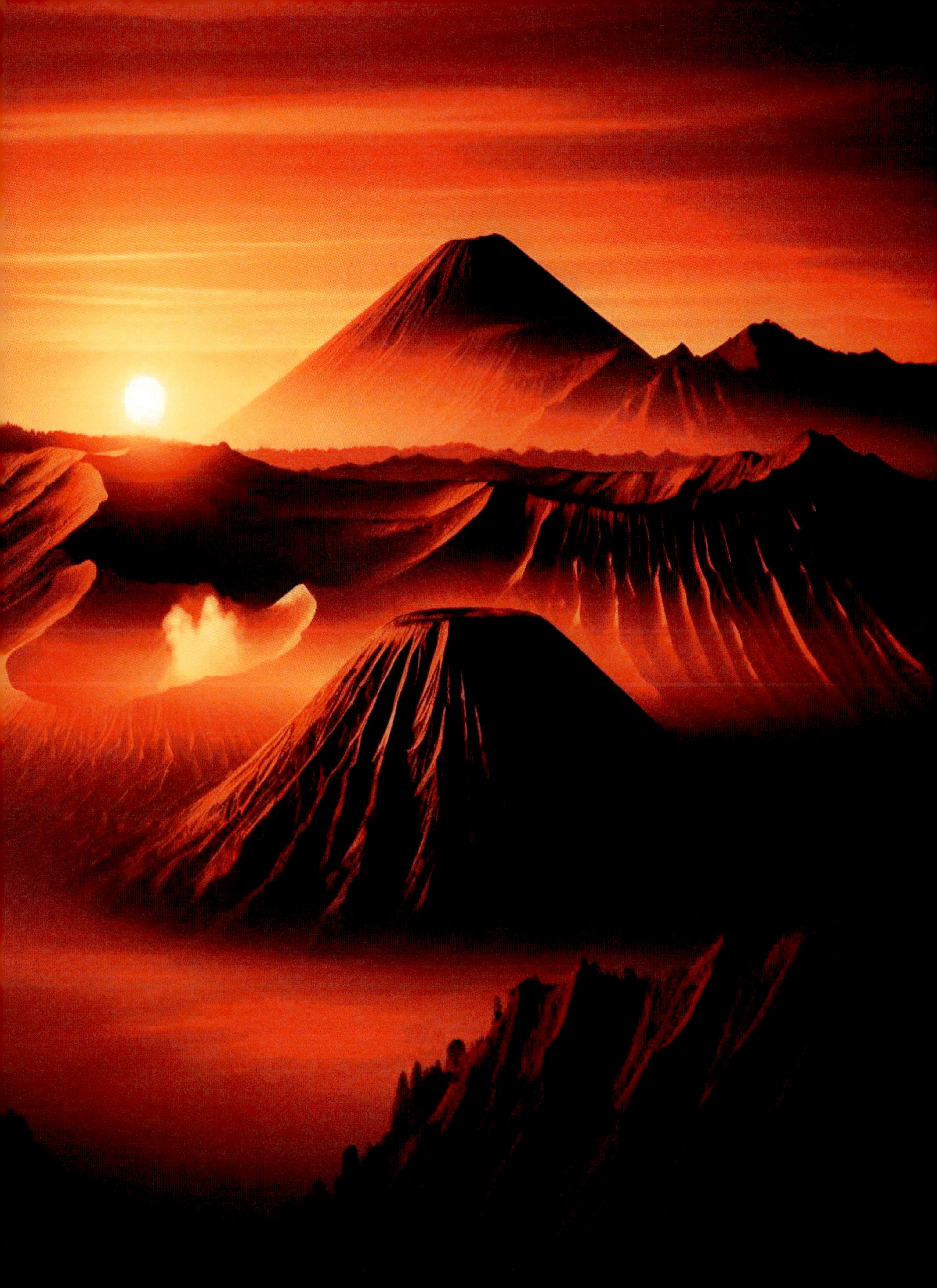

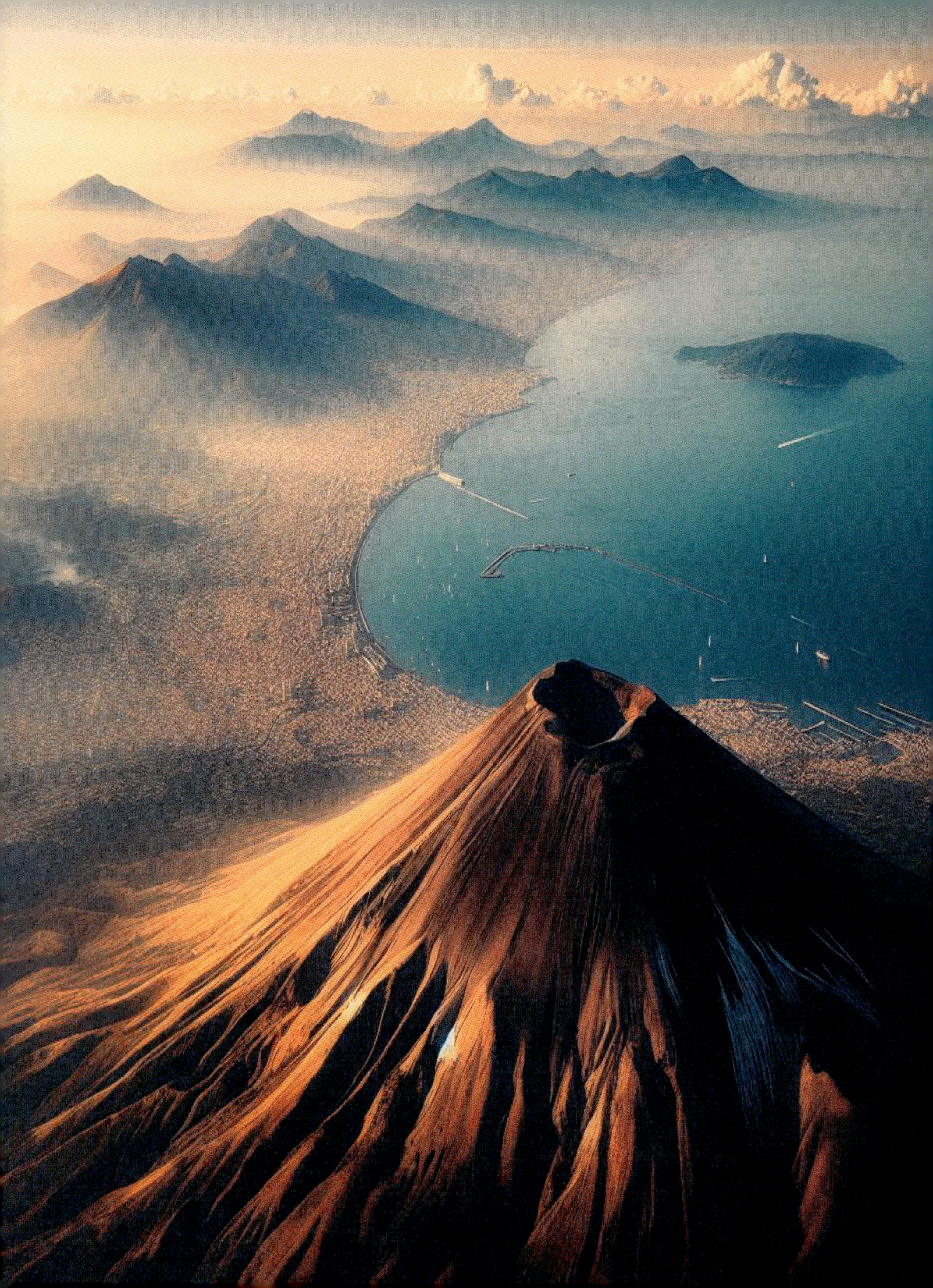

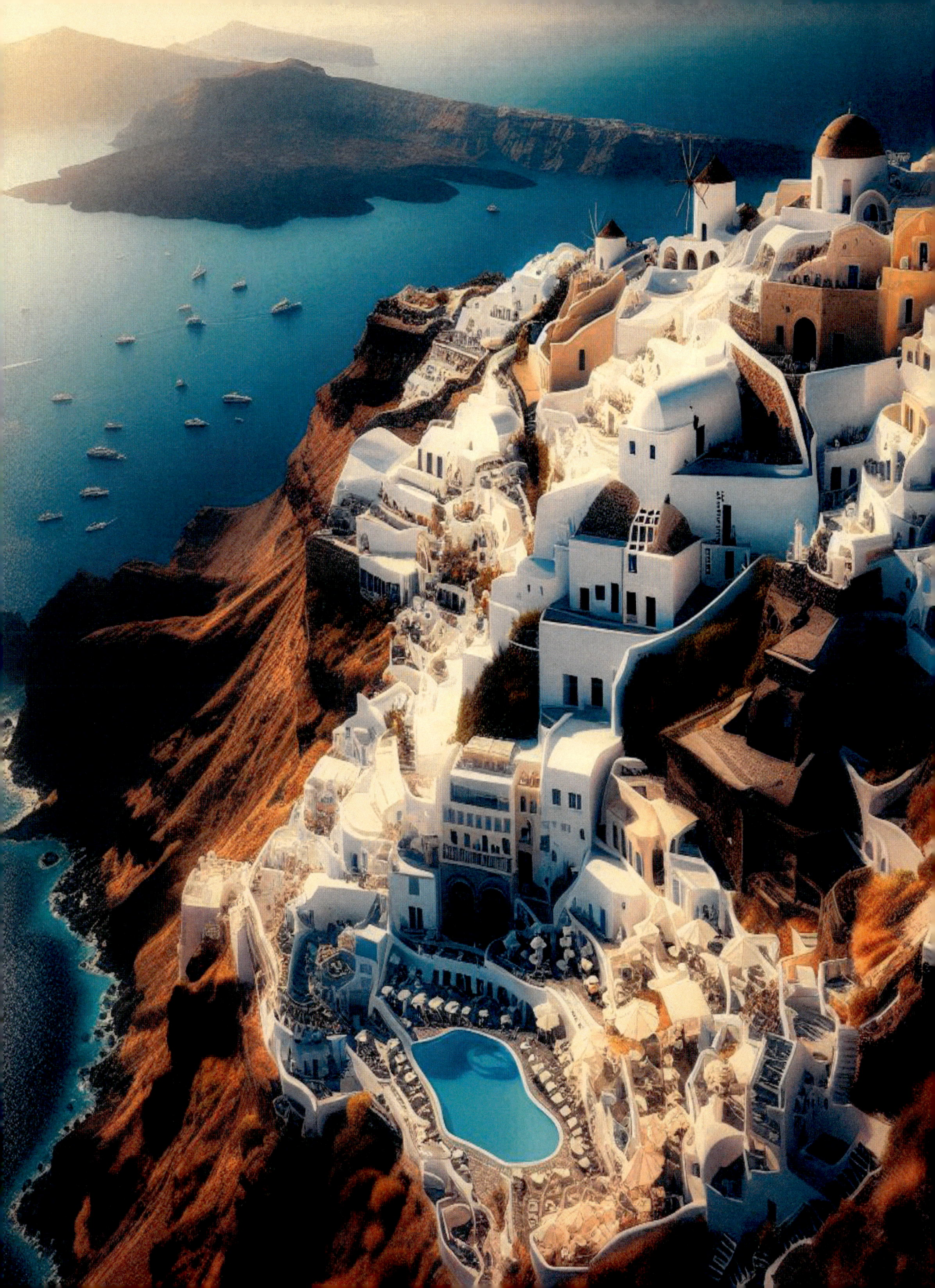

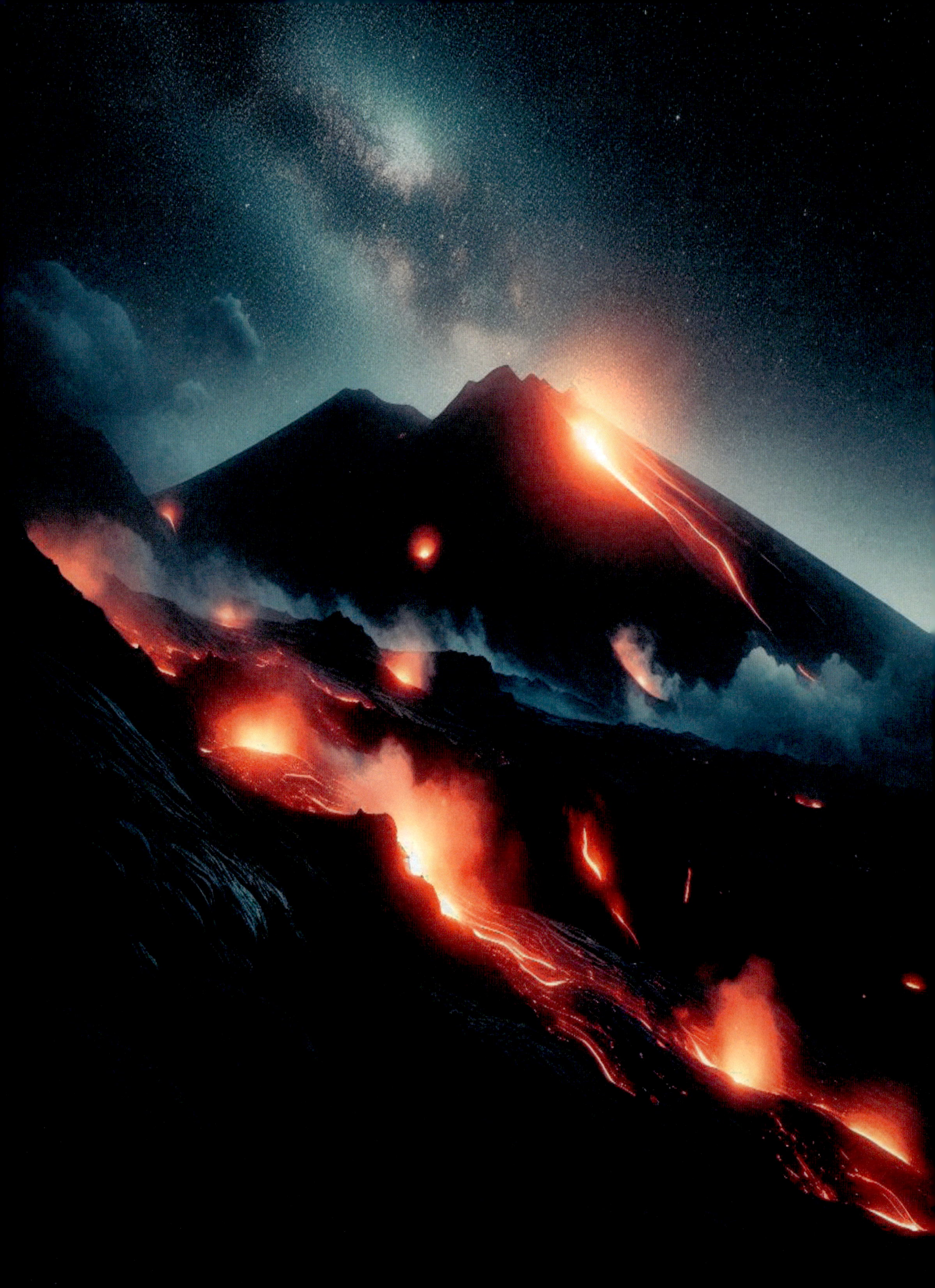

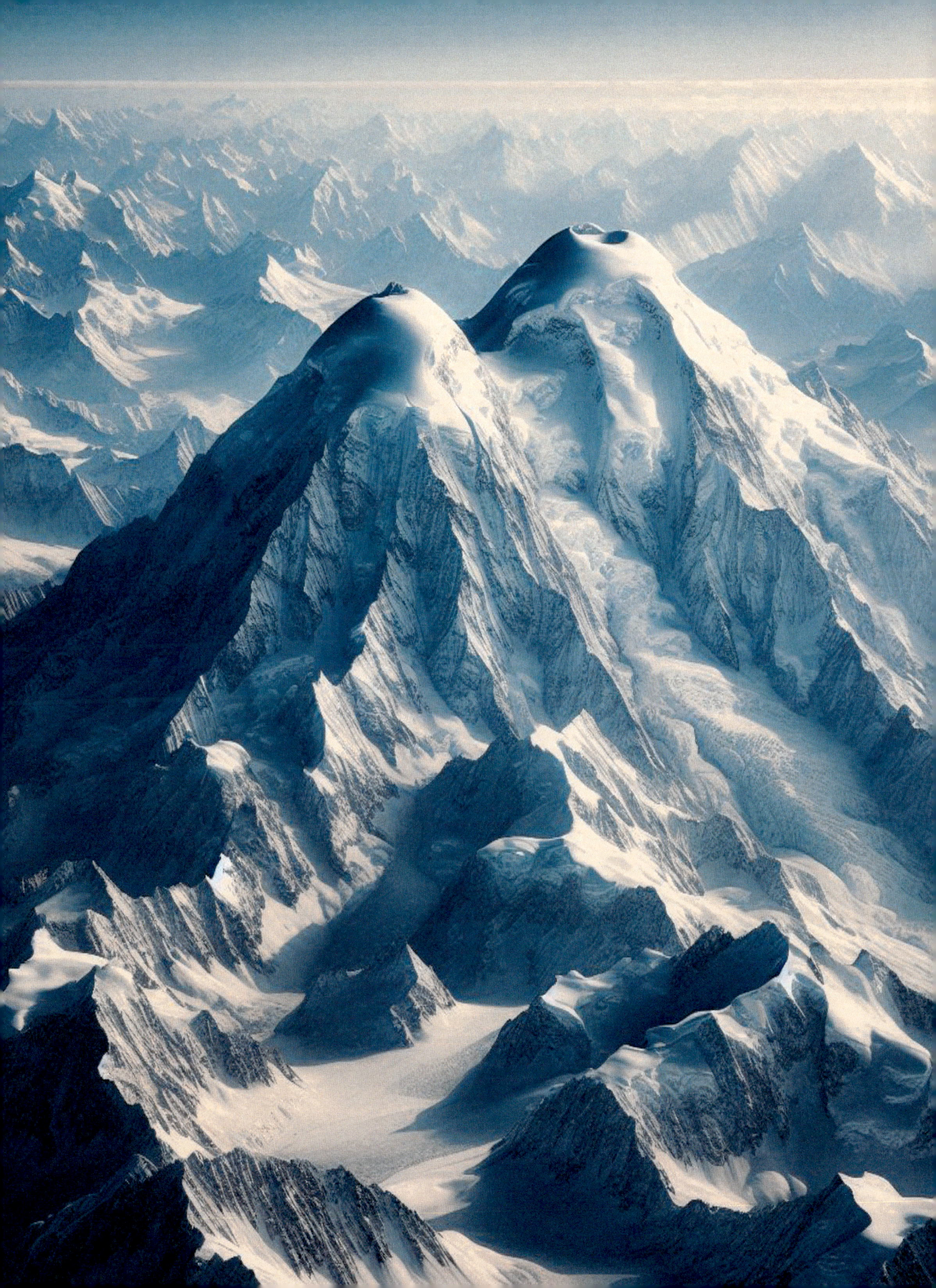

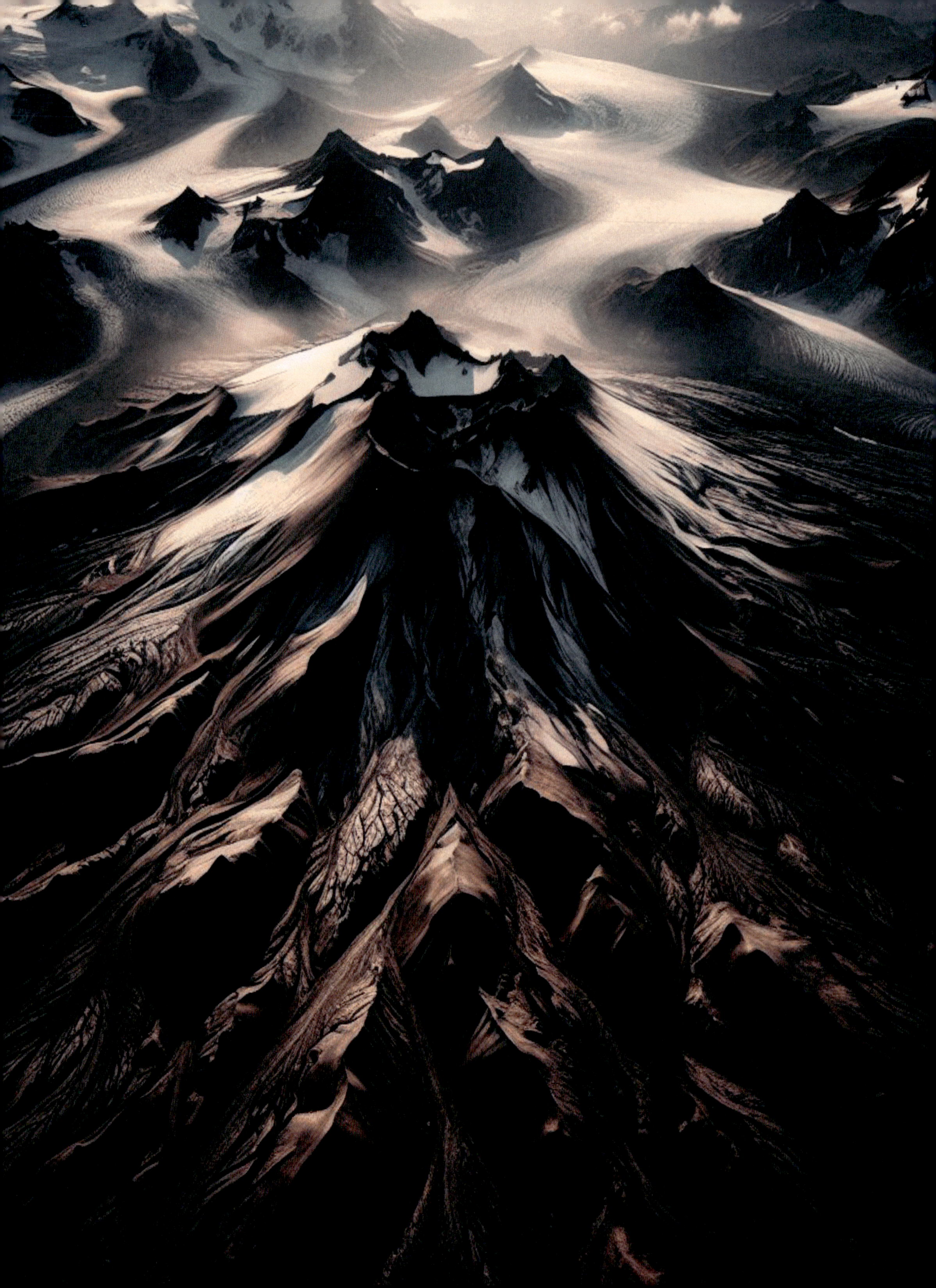

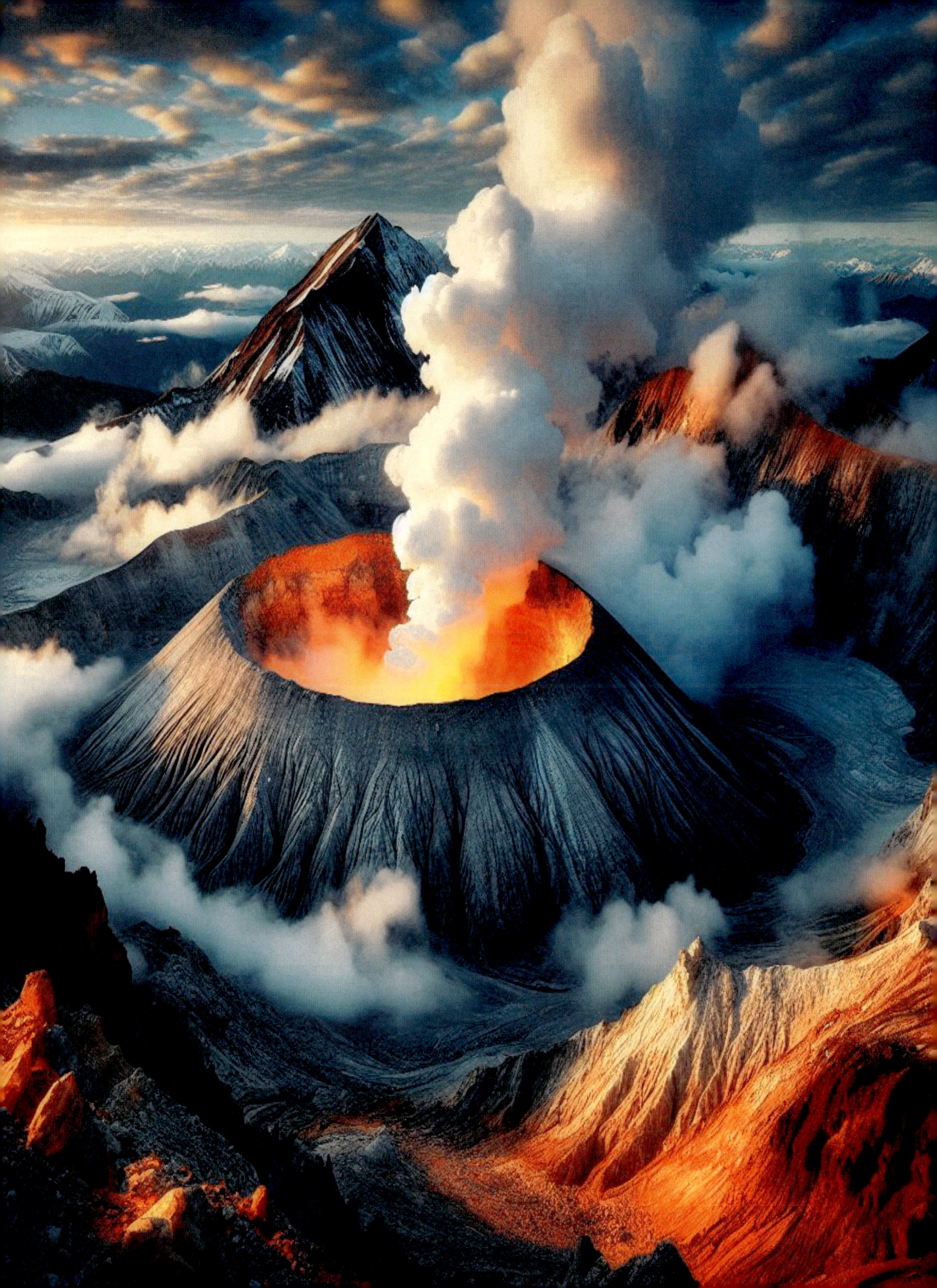

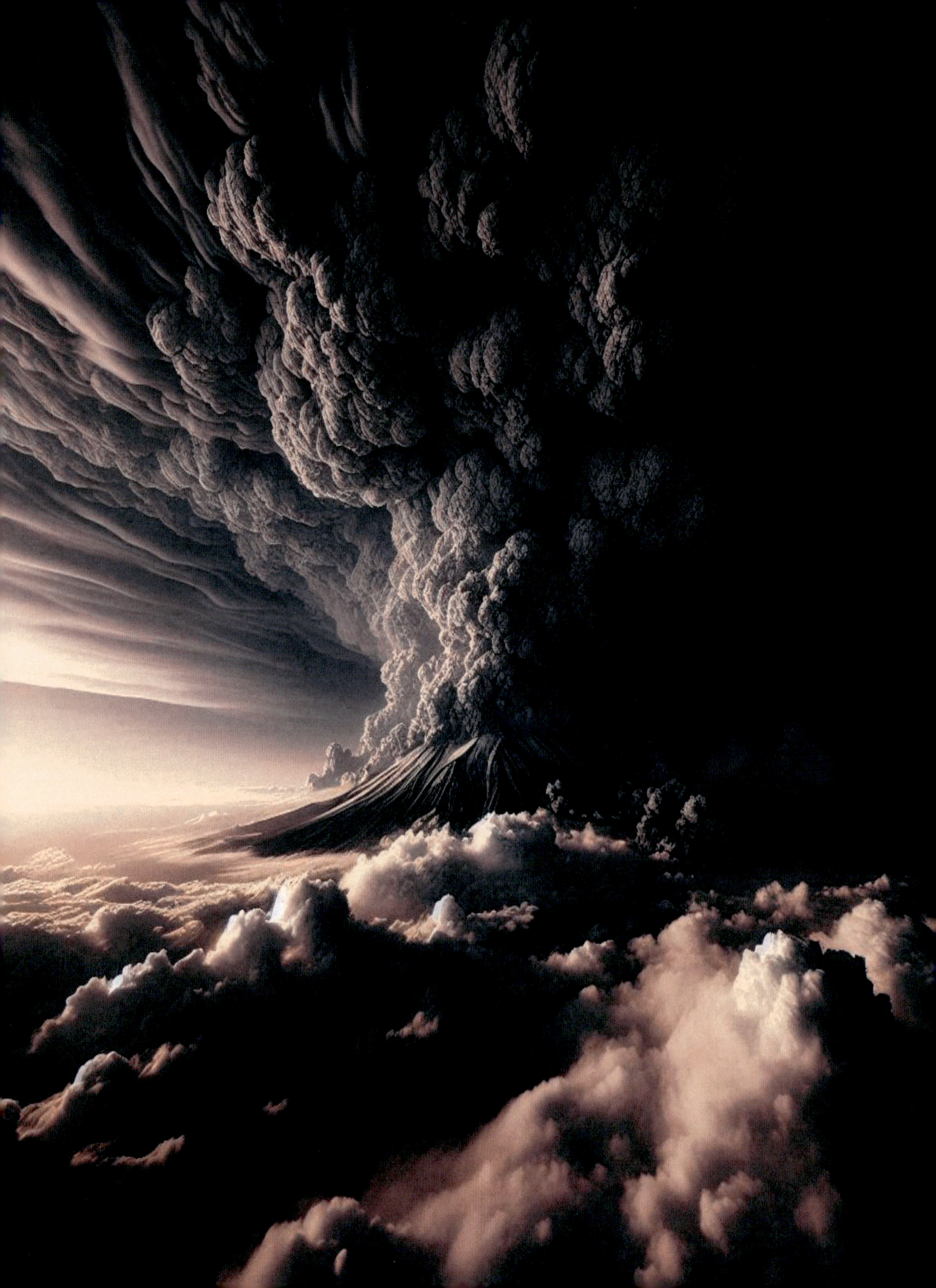

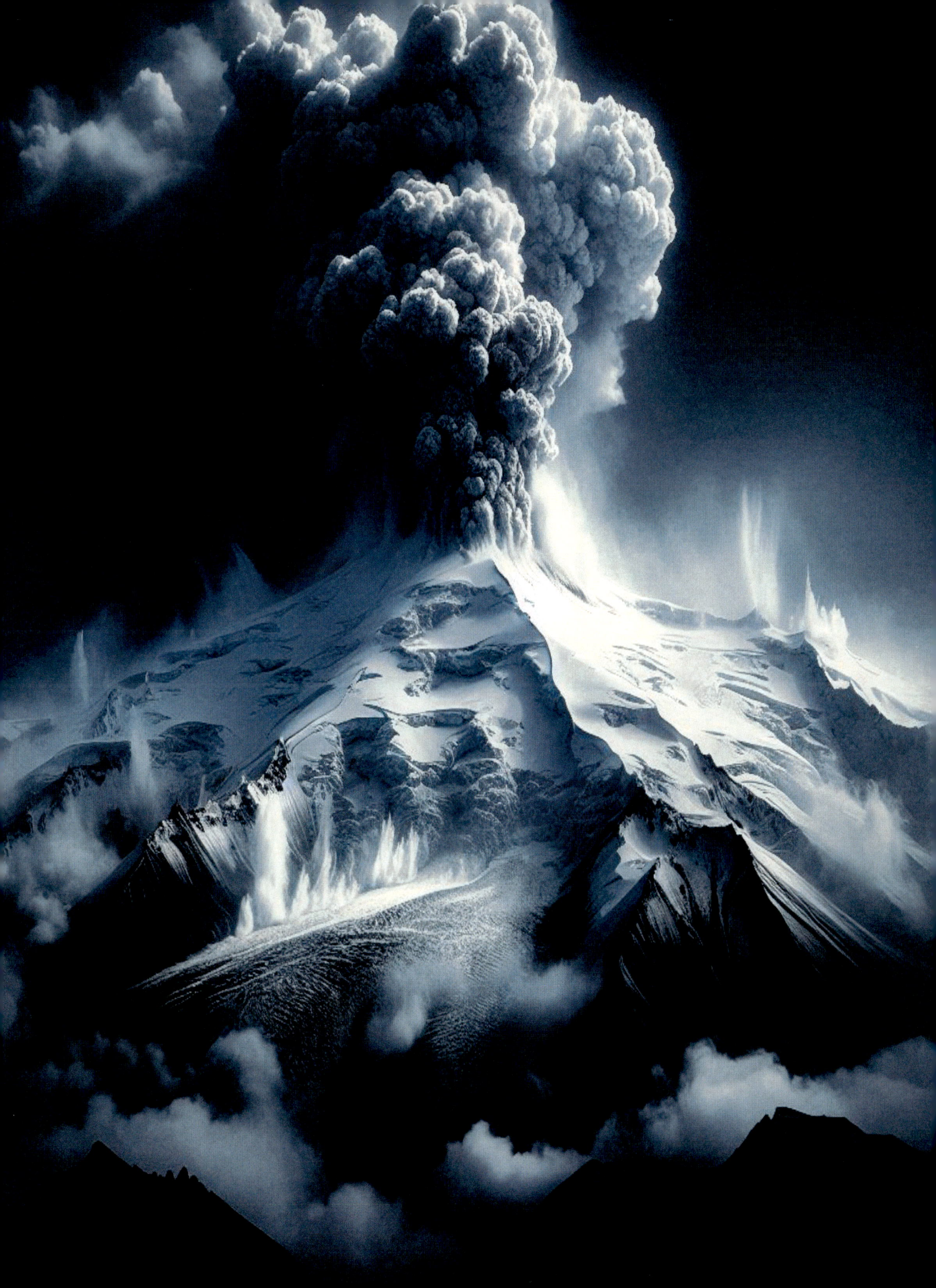

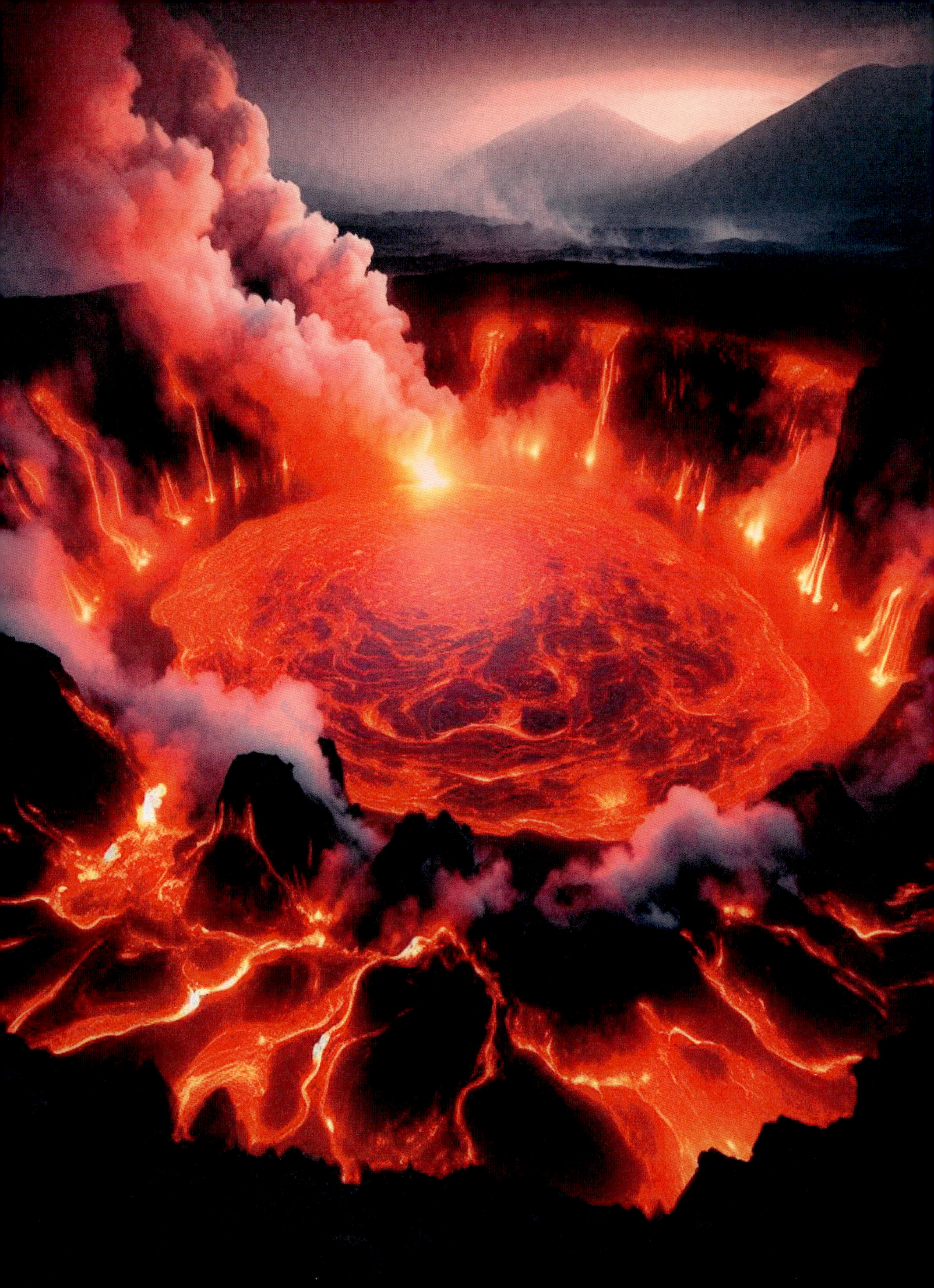

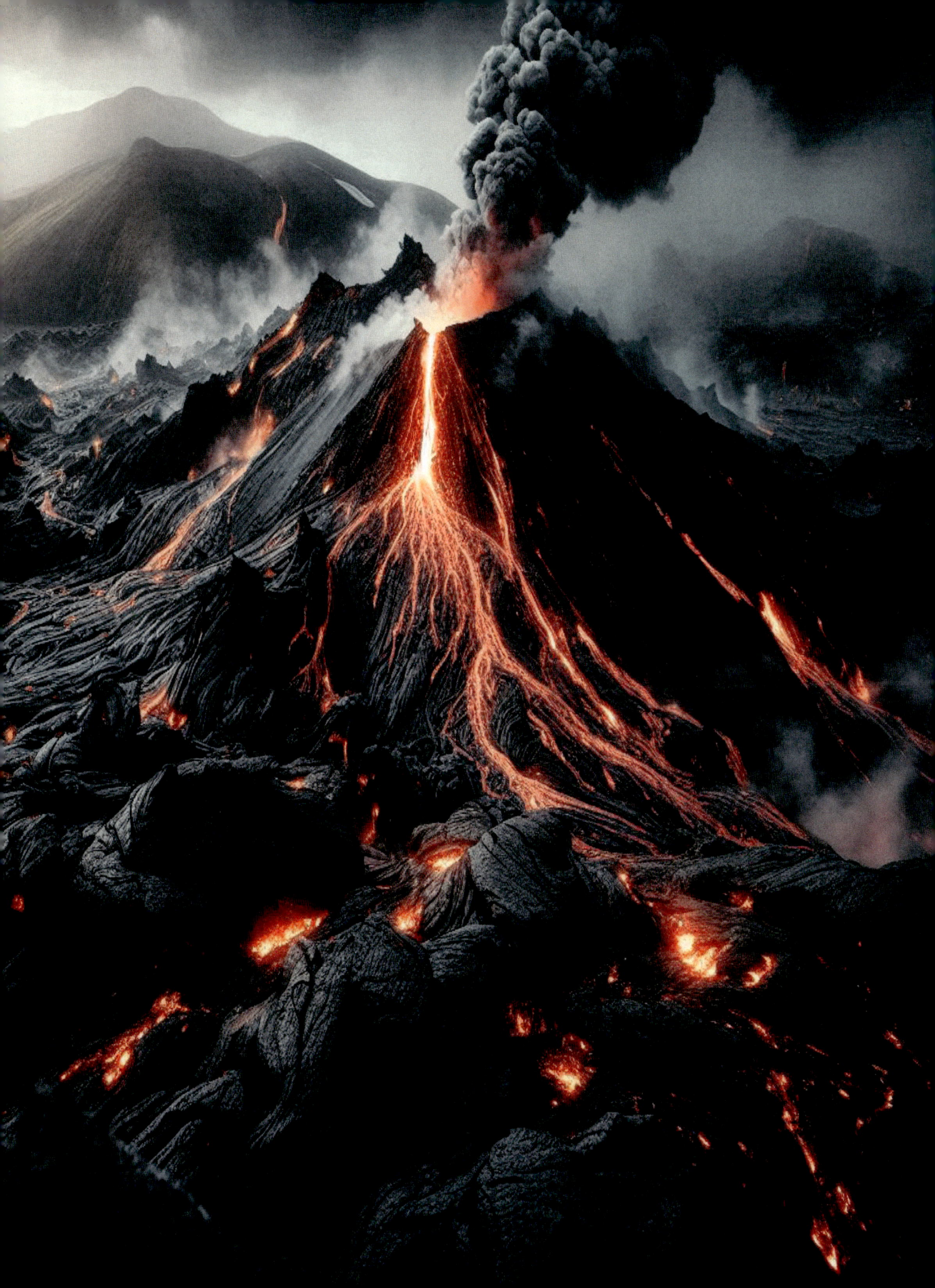

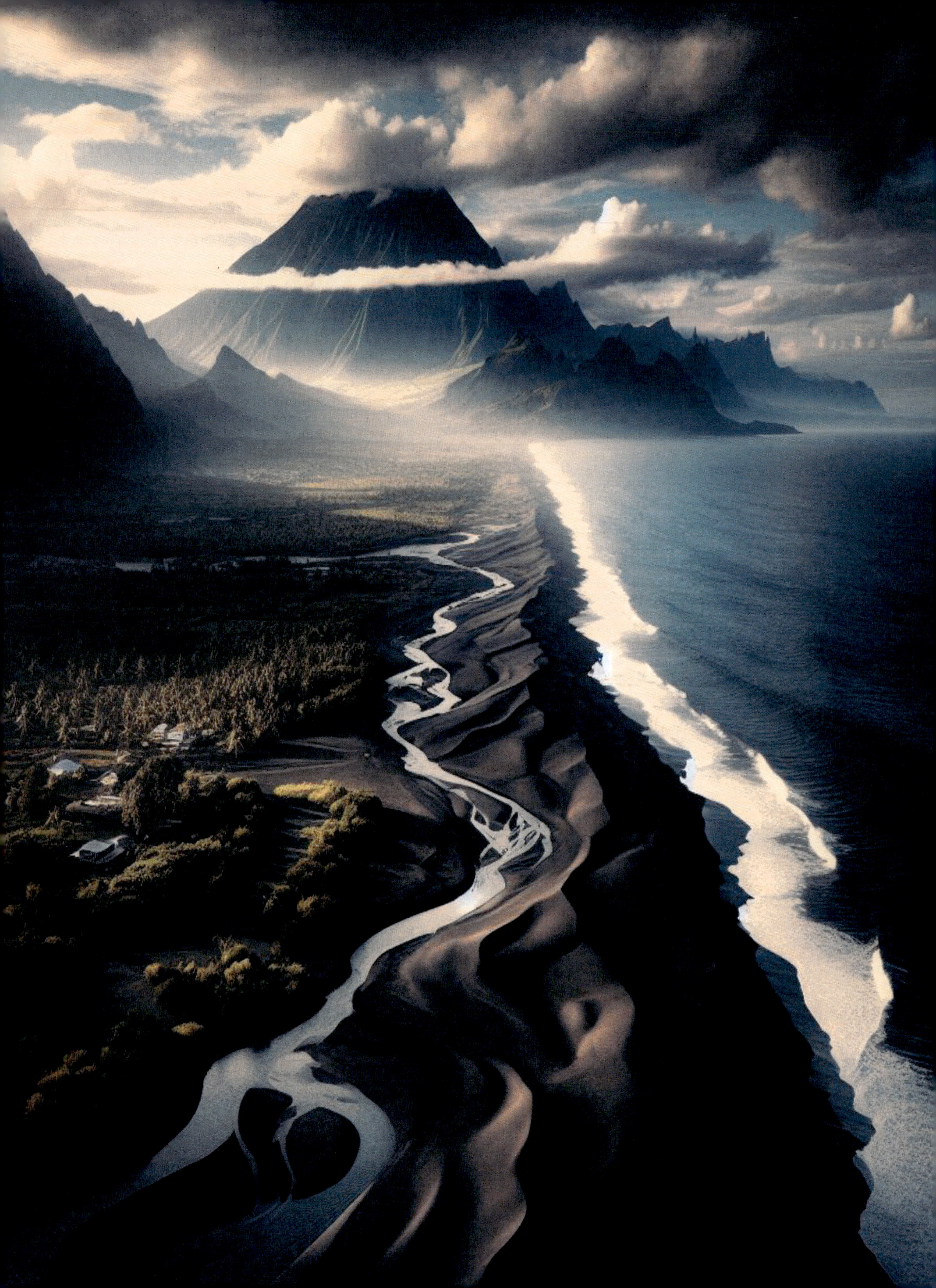

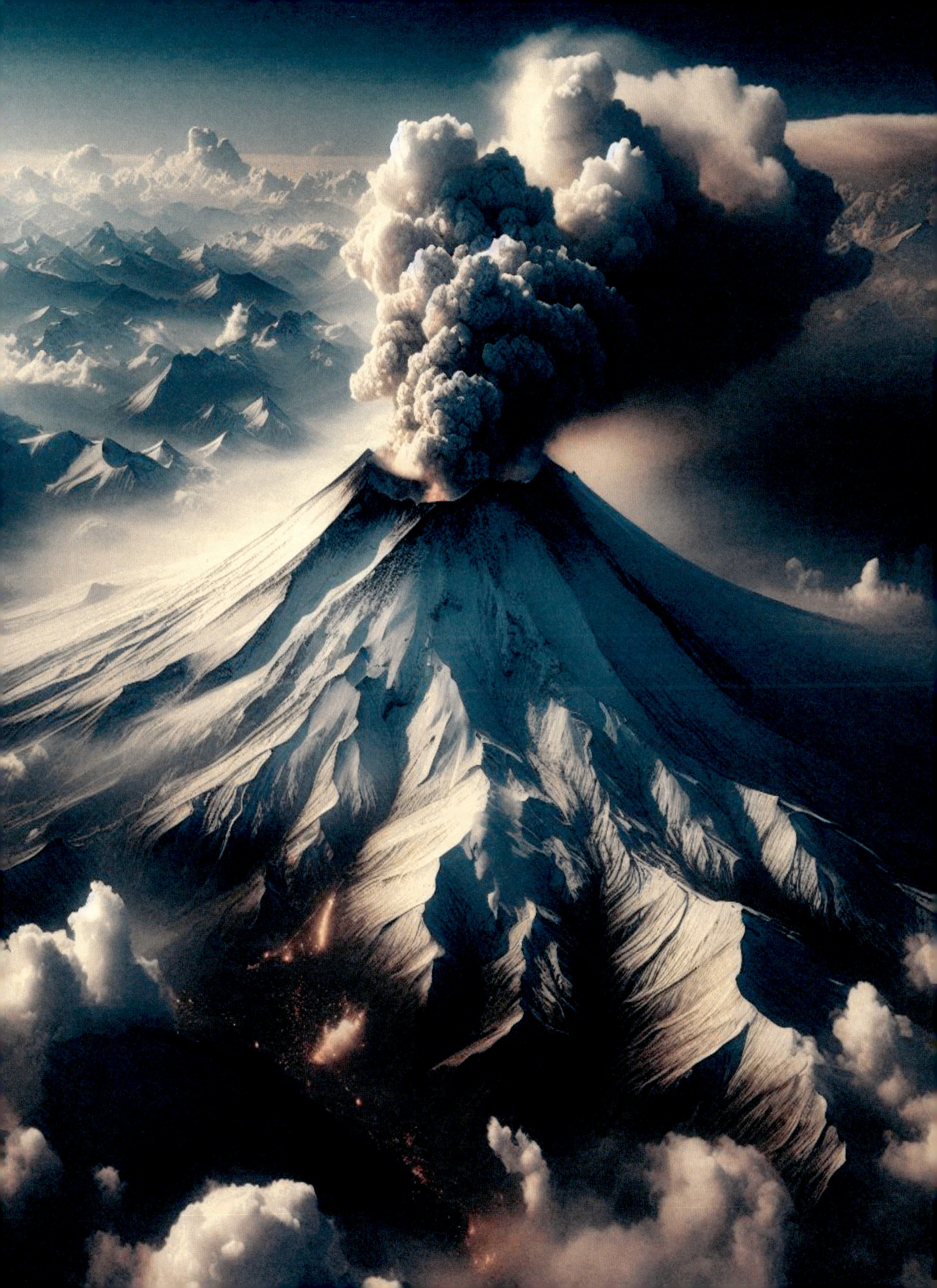

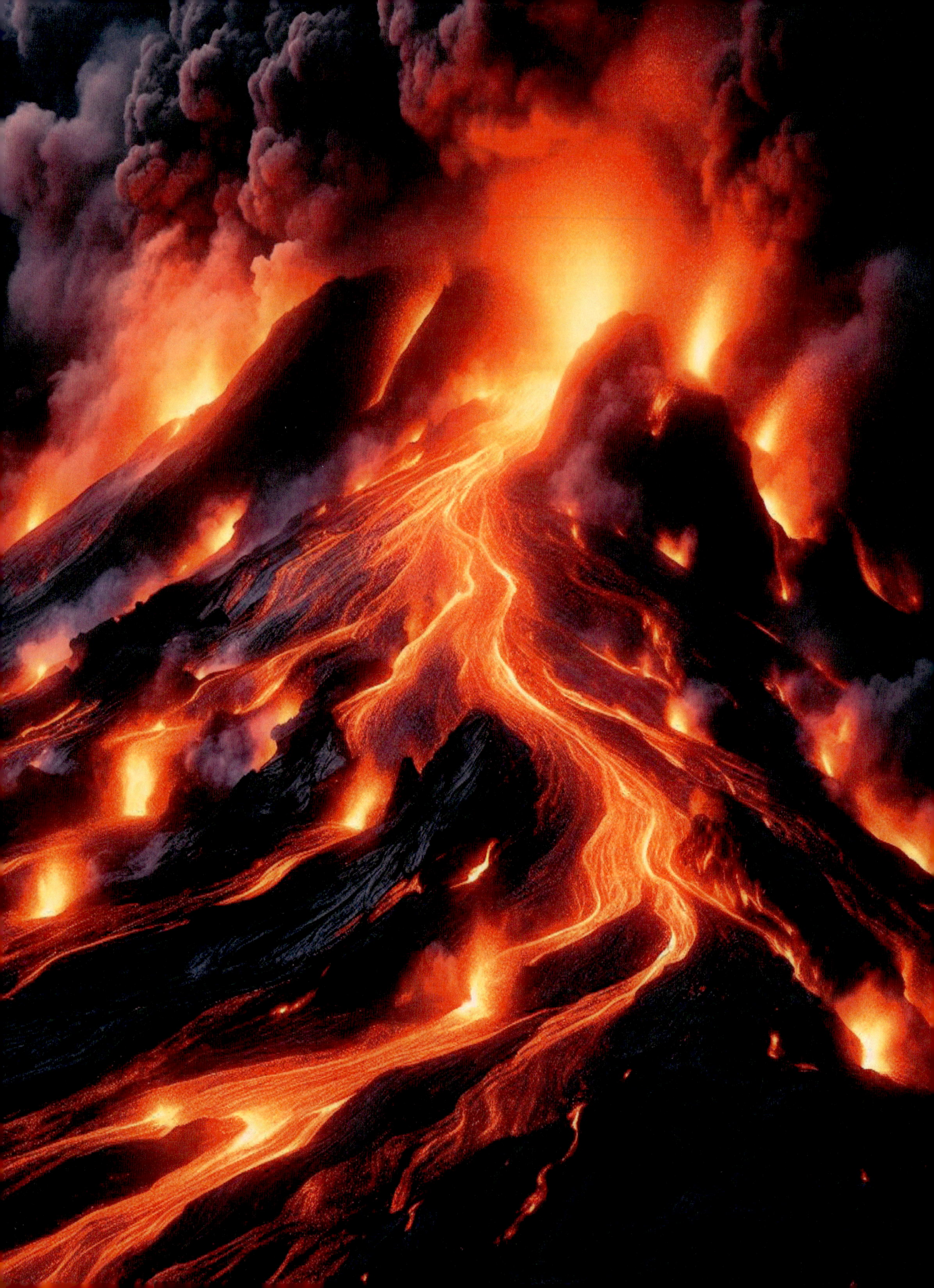

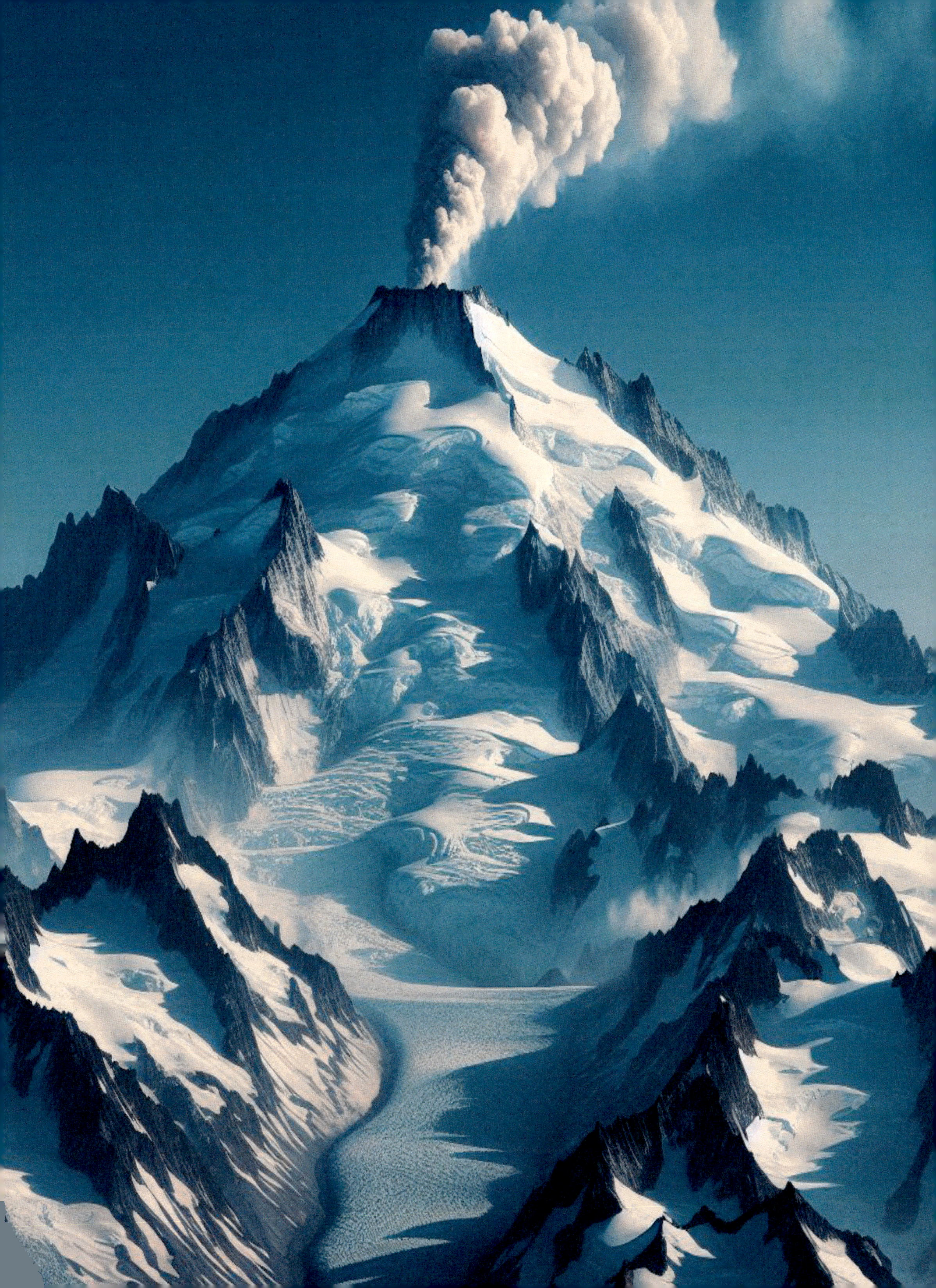

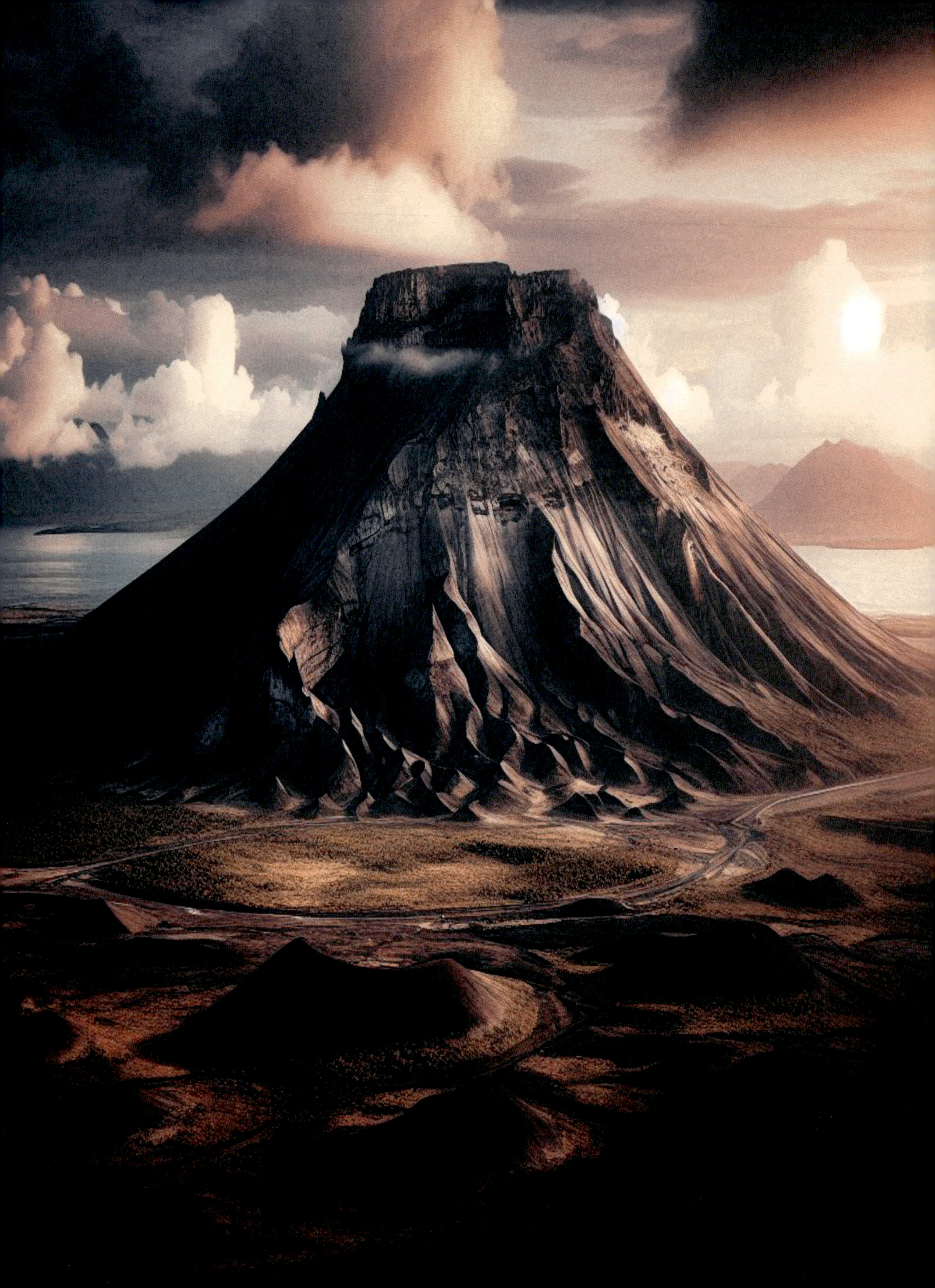

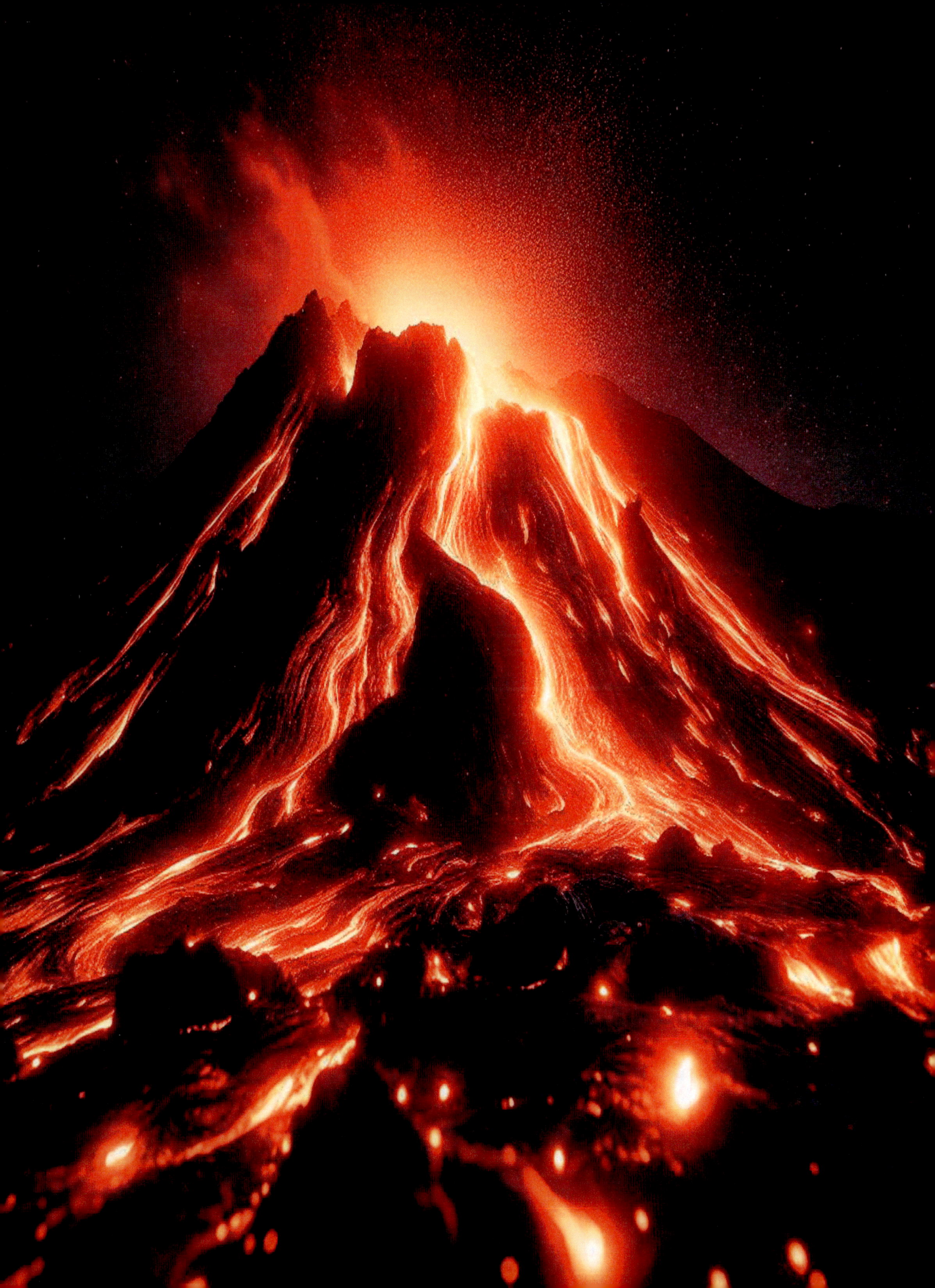

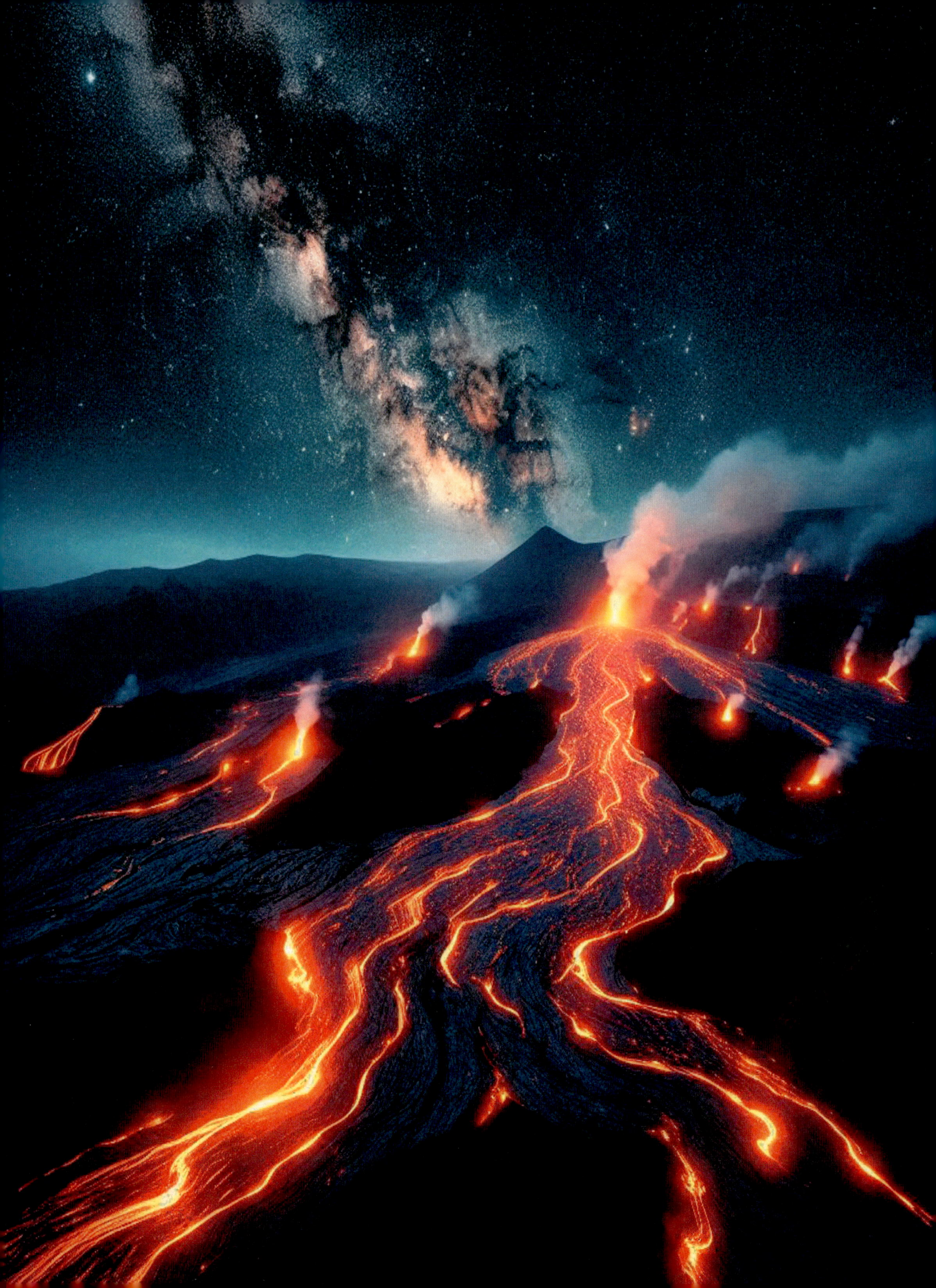

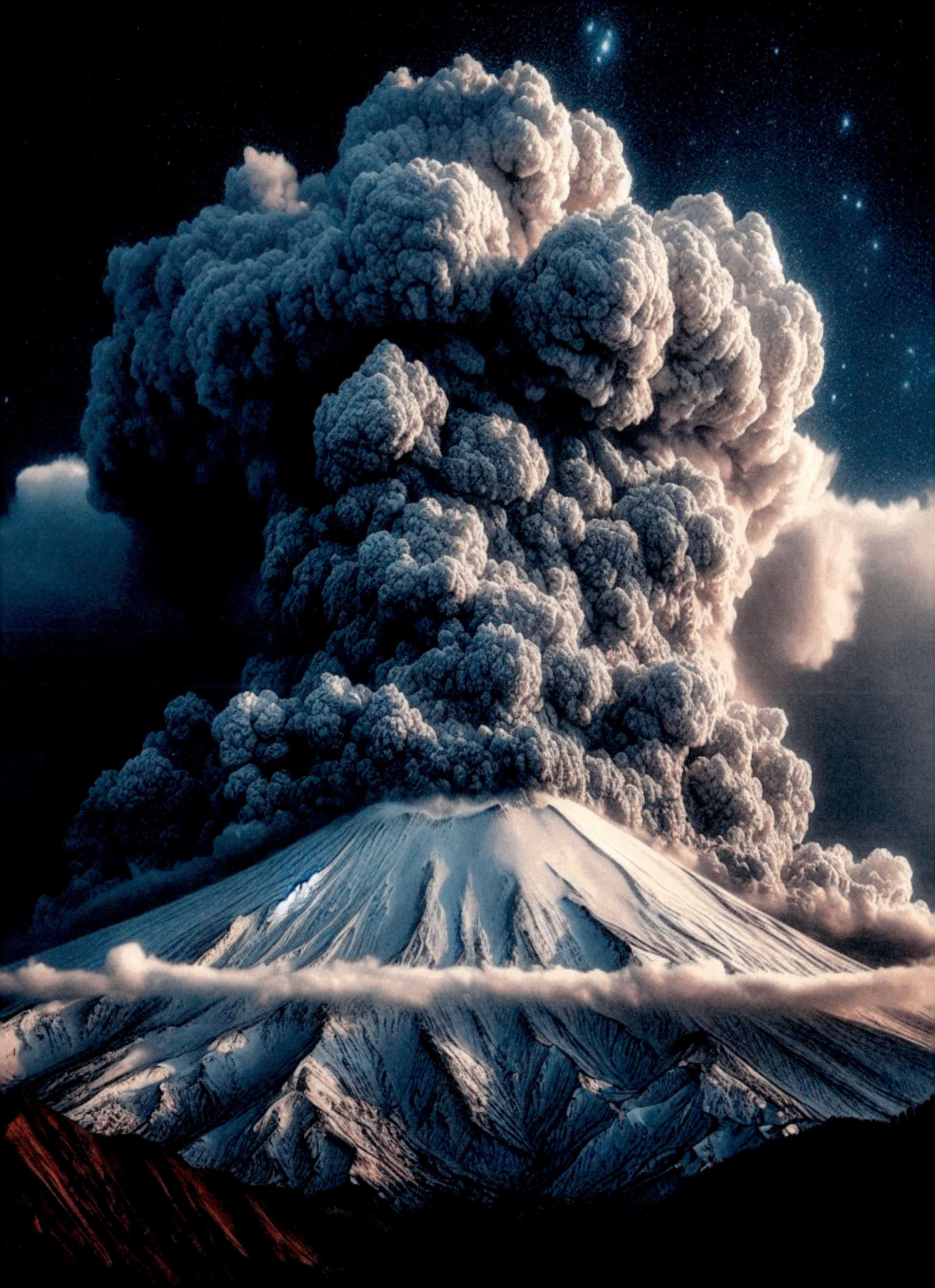

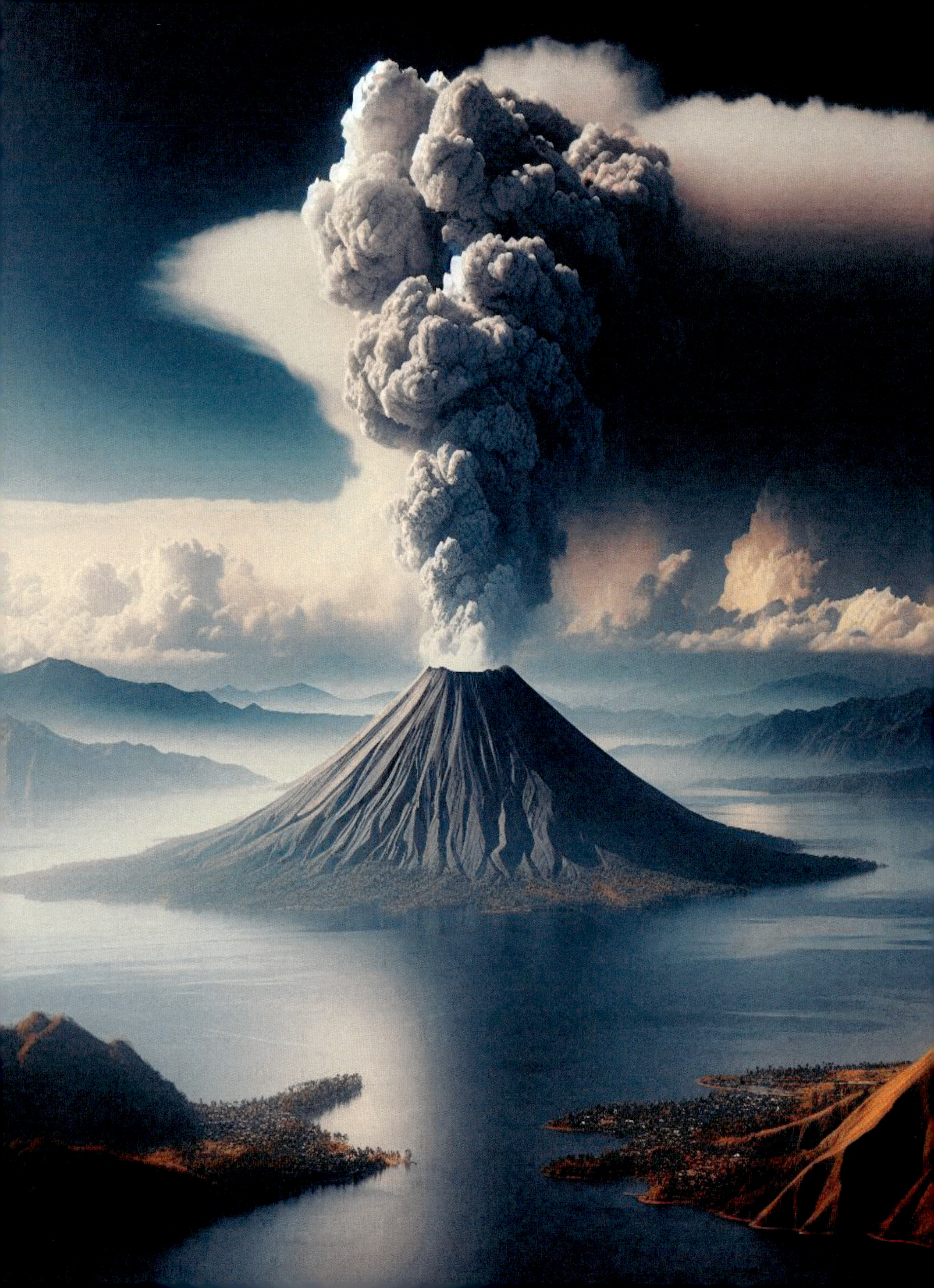

Made in the USA
Monee, IL
04 December 2024